CYNTHIA MONROE

LOVE
LIFTED ME

ANOINTED FIRE HOUSE™

Love Lifted Me
by Cynthia Monroe

© 2017, Cynthia Monroe
www.iamCynthiaMonroe.com
Cynthia_Monroe1@outlook.com

Published by Anointed Fire™ House
www.anointedfirehouse.com
Cover Design by Anointed Fire™ House
Author photograph by Citadel Nicolas

ISBN-10: 0-9982507-6-7
ISBN-13: 978-0-9982507-6-2

I have tried to recreate events, locales and conversations from my memories of them. In order to maintain their anonymity in some instances I have changed the names of individuals and places, I may have changed some identifying characteristics and details such as physical properties, occupations and places of residence.

Although the author and publisher have made every effort to ensure that the information in this book was correct at press time, the author and publisher do not assume and hereby disclaim any liability to any party for any loss, damage, or disruption caused by errors

Dedication

To God: the Father, Son, and Holy Spirit: I
dedicate this book to You. Receive it as my seed
sown into the earth for the work of your
Kingdom. Let this book increase Your family and
bring You glory.

Table of Contents

Acknowledgments

Thank you, Holy Spirit. Without Your leading and inspiration, this book would never have come forth.

My mother, Lydia: Thank you for loving me when I was unlovable and displaying what a true woman of God is through your actions.

My step-father, Robert: Thank you for choosing to be a father to me and refusing to give up on that job even when I was in my darkest hours. You loved me in my mess.

To my four blessings from the Lord (my children): Anthony, Andrew, Julian, and Elizabeth: You believed in me when it looked like I wasn't coming out of the darkness and you prayed for me when I seemed to be getting worse. Your love kept me going, and when I was in my pit, it was your faces that brought me hope. You inspired me to somehow get out of my madness so that I could love you all the more. Now, look at what God has done. Always remember this one thing, "With men, this is impossible; but with God all things are possible."

To my aunt, Norma, and my uncle, Daniel: Thank you for prayers and constant support.

To Erika, Natty, Marlene, Linda and all the other women God sent into life to be my sisters-in-Christ: Thank you for encouraging me to write this book. Thank you for never judging me, but always loving me. Thank you for rallying around me and speaking life to me when I was weary and thank you for believing in what God promised He would do in my life.

Pastor Joel and Pastor Kathie: Thank you for being true shepherds and genuine examples of what God's love in action truly looks like. When I felt there was no love available in the church, your love literally loved me back into the Kingdom of God.

To my loyal friend, Monique: You stuck by me when most friends would have left a messed up girl like me alone. You never judged me; instead, you've always protected my dignity, stood up for me, and loved me unconditionally. Thank you and I love you.

To Tiffany, my editor and publisher: Thank you

for being my spiritual midwife and helping in the "birthing process" of this book.

To all that prayed for me in my addiction and stood in the gap for me: I thank God for you.

To everyone who helped make this book: I appreciate you. Thank you for speaking the Word of the Lord over me when I was weary in writing and thank you for pushing me towards my goal. Your love has forever made an impact on my life. I love you all.

Introduction

I am a woman of God. I can say that with all certainty now, but at one point in my life, this statement was far from the truth. I was once better described as a child of disobedience. I wasn't born that way though; none of us are. Every single one of us is created in the image and likeness of God.

"So God created man in his own image, in the image of God created he him; male and female created he them."
Genesis 1:27 (NIV)

The enemy hates this fact. He will try his best to deceive people into thinking otherwise. He will whisper so subtly in our ears that we will think what we're hearing is coming from our own minds and our own thoughts. He will tell us that we were born to be failures or worst, that our births were a mistake. This is a lie that came straight from hell. God knew you from the beginning of time and always had a plan for your life.

"I knew you before I formed you in your mother's womb. Before you were born I set you apart."
Jeremiah 1:5 (NIV)

In the pages that follow, I'm going to share my testimony and my story of deliverance with you. It is an account of my journey through the wilderness from a child of God who knew and served Him, but made a choice to fully turn from His ways. I abandoned the call on my life and willingly chose to become a child of disobedience. I will talk about the destruction that came with that choice and the broken condition that it left me in. After that, I will testify to the amazing grace and mercy that the Lord extended to me at the lowest point of my life. God transformed this broken vessel into the woman of God I am today.

"Come and hear, all you who fear God, and I will tell what he has done for my soul."
Psalm 66:16 (ESV)

As you read my testimony of deliverance, I pray that it ministers to your heart and brings hope to all who read it.

CHAPTER 1

The Darkest Hour is Before Dawn

As I lay in my bed, I still had the taste of charcoal in my mouth. It was early one August morning and my body was sore. I wasn't sure if it was because I had fallen down or because my stomach had been pumped the night before. Either way, I honestly didn't care. I was still alive. This was my second attempt to end my life in two months, but once again, I'd failed to end my life. As this reality began to kick in, I quickly reached over to the other side of the bed for the only thing I knew that would ease the overwhelming pain that I felt on the inside; I reached for my bottle of vodka. As I unscrewed the top, I took a long hard drink and before it could even hit me, I hated myself all over again. Questions flooded my mind. I despised what I had become and I felt so alone. I wanted it all to end, but every attempt I had made to kill myself had failed and the feeling of failure was overwhelming. I had failed at life. I'd failed my family, my friends, and my children; I couldn't even succeed at ending my own life. I couldn't figure out why I was still living. I wanted to die more than anything. I had given up on myself and I wished my family would do the same, but they refused. Especially my mother; my mother's love for me was relentless. As I lay in my bed, I tried to make sense of it all. I couldn't see any good left in my life. I had two failed marriages and I'd failed the ministry God called me to because I'd walked away from it. My children had abandoned me and the sheer hell that I went through in the past eight years of my life was unbearable. Life wasn't always this way, I recalled. I wasn't always an alcoholic. I couldn't go without a drink for more than an hour without getting the shakes. What happened to me? I reached over again for the bottle as I tried to drown out any emotions that tried to rise up.

I'm going to take you to the beginning, way back to the year of 1976. My mother told me that on the day that she went into labor with me, she was getting ready for her eight hour shift at the hair salon. This was on Valentine's Day of 1976. She was in labor all day long, but gave birth to me 15 minutes after midnight on February 15, 1976. I was told that when I was born, I was so small that they (my aunts) put me inside a shoe box and carried me around like a baby doll. As for my father, he was not present at the time of my birth. He was serving in the Marine Corps overseas in Okinawa, Japan. He left when my mom was a few months pregnant, and although the Vietnam War had already ended when I was born, my father did not return home to meet me until I was over a year old. My mother told me that when I met my dad for the first time, I screamed and cried when he picked me up. She said that this was very awkward for my father, but what could he expect? I did not know him; he was a complete stranger to me.

My father had a difficult time adjusting to life after the war. Being thrown into the role of fatherhood at the same time was also quite overwhelming. My father was always a very spontaneous person. My mother said this is one of the things that attracted her to him. He was always on the go and he was always the life of the party. He enjoyed life to the fullest and was known for always being fun. He definitely wasn't used to being "tied down" in any way. He was known for his spontaneity. He would jump up and go for weekend getaways on a whim or ride his motorcycle on long road trips. He loved to ride up the coast of California with my mom on the back, pregnant and all. Needless to say, when I came into the picture, all that came to a halting end. This, along with other issues, put a strain on my parents' marriage. Shortly after my third birthday, my father moved out of our home, leaving my mom to care for me by herself. I am an only child, so it was just my mom and I. I was too young to fully comprehend what was happening. I didn't understand what separation or divorce was, but I did understand that my dad was gone and I missed him very much. I felt so rejected by him when he left. I didn't understand that he and my mom were having problems; all I knew was that my dad had left me. I also knew that my mom was always sad, because I would hear her crying at night when I was supposed to be asleep. Although I was very young, I vividly remember feeling that whatever caused my family to fall apart was my fault. I believed my father leaving was my fault and I believed that my mother's tears were because of my actions. That is the first memory I have of dealing with the spirit of rejection, but definitely would not be the last.

The spirit of rejection is a strongman or gatekeeper by which other demonic spirits enter in. Of course, at the time, I didn't know I was dealing with a demonic spirit; after all, I was a child. I simply believed that if I had behaved better, my dad would have stayed and whatever it was that my parents were fighting about all the time had to be my fault. I even believed that I was a bad child. In fact, I believed I was so bad that my dad wanted to get as far away from me as possible. The enemy saw an opportunity with me at a very young age and he jumped on it. This is one of his tactics. He uses traumatic events in a person's life, for example, divorce or a parent abandoning his or her child, to sow seeds in that child's life. These events serve as open doors by which demonic spirits such as rejection and other spirits that come in with the strongman of rejection like hurt, deep hurt and even shame enter in a child's life.

> *"But while men slept, his enemy came and sowed tares among the wheat, and went his way."*
> *Matthew 13:25 (KJV)*

The word *tares* in the Greek is the word *zizanion* (*G2215 - zizanion - Matthew 13:25 Strong's Greek Lexicon, KJV*). It is described as a "false grain" or something that resembles good grain, but when it matures, it brings forth grains that are black. These grains are not edible. In other words, it is unfruitful; it can even overtake the good grain and cause it not to yield its full harvest. Other bible translations translate this word as "weeds." I believe that this scripture is referring to anything that the enemy sows into our lives to choke out the plans and purposes that God has called us to and preordained for us, even before we were in our mother's wombs. That is the very purpose of these demonic spirits. They've come to hinder the call on a person's life and that person's God-given destiny.

So while my parents were caught up in a vortex of their own pain ... a pain that came from the hurt of their failing marriage, they were oblivious to the fact that the enemy was busy at work sowing hurt and destruction into their baby girl. The enemy sowed tares of rejection, hurt, shame and even anger into my life. I have found that this is often the case with people who have been set free from addictions and experienced deliverance in several areas in their lives. Many say that they can remember an event or a course of events they experienced in early childhood that "triggered" feelings of rejection or abandonment. These events are what led them to acting out later on in life.

"But when the blade was sprung up, and brought forth fruit, then appeared the tares also."
Matthew 13:26 (KJV)

It never ceases to amaze me that people really believe the devil fights fair. This is not so. The enemy is described in the bible as a "roaring lion" who roams the earth, looking for those to deceive, lead to destruction and devour (1 Peter

5:8). An innocent child is the most vulnerable target, especially when the parents are unaware or too wrapped in their own hurts to recognize the enemy's schemes. Just as the scripture says, it's not until later on when those tares and weeds spring up that the enemy's work is visible. That's why as parents, our job is to cover our children in prayer. We must war in the spirit for them and protect them from the adversary. This is the part of godly parenting that is of the utmost importance. We must not be passive concerning our children, for the enemy sees our passivity as another way to get a foothold into their lives .We must know our adversary and understand how he operates if we want to be strategic prayer warriors.

Chapter 2

California, to the Riverwalk, Back to Gamble Street

After my parents divorced, my mother and I moved from California to Texas in an attempt to start a new life. We moved in with my dad's family in San Antonio temporarily. Eventually, my mom landed a job as a property manager and we lived on-site in a nice townhouse. This was a tough time for me and my mom. We were far away from our family in California and I was far away from my dad.

My mother worked very hard just to make ends meet and sometimes, we had very little to eat. Shortly after I celebrated my fifth birthday, we packed up of the few belongings that we had and moved back to California. I was thrilled to be headed back home to be with my family and to see my dad again.

When we returned to California, we moved to Escondido, California. We moved in with my grandmother on a street called Gamble Street.

I have wonderful memories of living there. I remember my cousins and I playing tag and hanging out with the other neighborhood kids. When I was about six years old, my mother and I moved to a nearby coastal city called Cardiff by the Sea; this was near San Diego. I loved living there. We had a tiny studio apartment and I remember that it was covered with avocado green shag carpet.

My mother would work full time as a hairdresser, go to college in the evenings, and on the weekends, she cleaned homes as a second job. The arrangement that my mom and dad had for visitation was set up this way: every other weekend, my father was to pick me up on Friday nights at six o'clock. I would return home on Sunday evening. I can still remember the knot I would get in the middle of my stomach during my kindergarten class on the Fridays that were my dad's weekends. I would anxiously watch the big clock in the back of classroom and count how long it would be until six o'clock. I felt this way partly because I was excited to see my dad but, for the most part, it was due to a nervous stomach. I was nervous because I didn't know if my dad would show up to pick me up. My father was notorious for standing me up on Friday nights. This was before we had cell phones, so the waiting game would be unbearable for me. I remember feeling the spirit of rejection rise up in me as I sat in the mall parking lot, sometimes for hours, waiting for him to show. I felt so rejected and ashamed. The thoughts that had taken root when I was younger would roll around in my mind, and they were some very terrible thoughts. I would hear things like, "Your dad doesn't care about you" or "Your dad doesn't even think you're worth showing up for." If my dad did show up, he was usually several hours late. Of course, he would always have a legitimate excuse, along with some new girlfriend on his arm. This only reinforced my beliefs. Those haunting thoughts would come back and I'd hear, "Your dad doesn't even love you. He loves his girlfriends more than you and that's why he would rather spend time with them than to spend time with you." Things didn't get any better after he picked me up. I spent the entire weekends with my dad constantly trying to grab his attention from these other women and put it back on me. I always felt like I had to compete for his attention. This made me feel like I held second place in his heart. After a while, I stopped competing for my father's attention. I just accepted the belief that I wasn't worthy or that I didn't deserve to have all his attention. I didn't realize it then, but this was exactly the enemy's plan. Those feelings of unworthiness followed me into my adult life and clouded my judgment when it came to other relationships. It also affected my self-esteem and self-image to a great degree. *A note to the fathers: please know that your role in your daughter's life is so very important. It goes far beyond just being present in her life; you must be an example of who her heavenly Father is and a constant reminder of His unconditional love for her.* I lacked this from my own father. The effects of this would not be fully evident until I was older when those tares and weeds sprang up.

CHAPTER 3

Good Times, Hard Times

After my parents divorced, my mother continued working both jobs and going to college at night. When I was about eight years old, she met a man and they began dating. When I was nine years old, they were married and our lives completely changed. My step-father was a wealthy man and my mom and I moved out of our little studio apartment in Cardiff to upscale Rancho Santa Fe. We moved into a beautiful home, located on a golf course. We literally went from rags to riches. For the first time in my life, we were happy. It wasn't solely due to money (even though that didn't hurt any), but it had everything to do with the type of man my step-father was. He was such a wonderful man. He treated my mother like a queen and me like a princess. I remember thinking that I had never seen my mother smile so much in my entire life. We had the kind of life that I thought only existed in movies or on television. We traveled to places I had never been to and experienced things I had only heard of. I continued to see my father every other weekend; that is, when he would show up. However, his actions and lack of attention towards me didn't seem to sting as much anymore, now that I had my step-father in the picture. With my stepdad, I always felt that I was his first priority. He was also very supportive of my mother's education. I have great memories of me and him spending time together while my mother studied.

My mom finished her schooling and graduated from college with her Master's Degree in Psychology when I was 11 years old. She began a private practice as a biblical psychologist and enjoyed it very much. My parents were very involved in the local church; we were active members of our community and I was active in the youth group. My life was good and it felt complete. Everyone loved my step-father. He was the kindest and most generous man I had ever known. He was a giver and loved the Lord with all his heart. For the first time in my life, I experienced what a family was supposed to be like and I loved every moment.

Shortly after my mother began working as a psychologist, my stepfather started having health issues. He suffered a stroke and as a result of that stroke, lost partial vision in his right eye. This was extremely tough. My stepfather, having been an independent man all his life, had trouble with the effects of his stroke. He was no longer able to drive and we had to assist him with walking. We weren't able to travel anymore and my stepdad became depressed. His health began to further deteriorate and he was in and out of the hospital. My youth group and youth pastor were very supportive of me during this time. The church was very supportive of my mother as well. My mom was caring for my stepfather full time at this point.

One day, while at school, I was called to the office. I was then told that my stepdad had to be taken to the hospital by an ambulance. He was very ill and suffered from congestive heart failure. After being in the hospital for about a week, he had a massive heart attack and died. This completely devastated both me and my mom. Words cannot describe the sadness that I felt when he died. I felt as though the rug had been pulled out from underneath me. I didn't understand why anyone as kind and loving as my stepfather had to die. Everybody was saddened by his death. My mom was in shock. She was so distraught. The smile that my stepfather had kept on my mom's face was now replaced by sadness and tears. I couldn't help but feel sorry for her. She had finally found the man of her dreams, only to have him ripped away from her.

I vaguely remember the funeral, but I do remember something that happened immediately after the funeral during the drive back home. My mom asked my aunt if they could take me to the reception back at our home. On the ride back, I was in the backseat of the car and I had my eyes closed. I wasn't crying, but I was very sad. I was trying to make sense of everything that was happening in my eleven-year-old mind. I was trying to process it all. I remember the feelings of rejection returning again. I felt so alone and rejected by my stepdad for leaving me. I knew it wasn't intentional. He didn't choose to die, but I felt abandoned once more nonetheless. The next thing I remember was the feeling of anger rising up in me. I was mad and wanted to blame God for my stepfather's death. I vividly remember a voice speaking to me at that very moment. It sounded as if someone was up close and speaking directly in my ear, but there was no one else in the backseat with me. I knew it wasn't my aunt or uncle speaking, because I could hear them talking to each other in the front seat. The voice said these words in a defiant tone: "You should get angry for what happened to your step dad. You deserve to get mad." The voice continued to say, "You prayed for him to get better and he didn't. God let you down and now, he is dead. You should get really angry and act really bad. Look at what being a nice Christian girl has gotten you ... nowhere. Your stepfather is dead and you and your mom are alone again. God doesn't care about you." I contemplated those words for a moment and then, I heard another voice. It was a soft voice; the very sound of it seemed to quiet the storm going on inside of me. The voice said, "Don't get angry; instead, get really involved in your youth group. Lean on your youth pastor and the others in your youth group to help you through this difficult time. Don't turn your back on God now. He is all you have." I remember making a definite decision that I would not get angry and I decided I would listen to the second voice.

Over the next few months, I threw myself into serving in my youth group. I participated in all the activities and was actively involved as much as I could be. I held on tight to my God and He comforted me the entire time. I was very sad when I found out that the house we lived in with my stepdad would have to be sold and we had to move back to Escondido. This was extremely hard for me because that meant leaving my youth group behind, but I remember thinking to myself that God wasn't stuck in one particular church building or in a certain youth group; He was everywhere. As soon as we moved back to Escondido, I got involved in a youth group right away. I held on tight to my faith in God. I honestly felt like He was the only thing that I had left. I had my mom, but she was still mourning the loss of my stepdad. I tried reaching out to my biological dad immediately after my stepdad passed away. I called him up and told him that I needed him and that I desired him to be more active in my life because I was hurting over my stepdad's death. His response was that he had just gotten engaged and would be moving in a few weeks. He was moving from San Diego, which was forty minutes from me, to a small town in northern California that was seven hours from me. Again, I felt rejected, pushed to the side and second in my dad's life. When I needed my dad the most, he would abandon me. Those negative thoughts flooded my mind once again and I couldn't understand why I wasn't good enough for him. Nevertheless, this time, I quickly dismissed them and I continued to hold on to God even tighter. My father moved shortly after that call. I would take a train up to see him once a year (during summer vacation); that was the extent of our relationship. My mother resumed her private practice of biblical counseling and we began to move forward in our lives. I began attending a private Christian school in my sixth-grade year. I was growing in the things of God, happy and loving my new youth group. Life was slowly beginning to get better—or so it seemed.

CHAPTER 4

Damaged Goods

When I was thirteen years old, the new youth group I was a part of was a mixture of teens, ages 13-17 years of age. Every month, our group would go down to Mexico on a mission's trip to a children's orphanage. It was something I anticipated attending every month. I so loved being a part of the mission's field. We would go to the same orphanage every month. We would bring clothing and toys to the precious children at the orphanage. We had the opportunity to feed them, read bible stories to them, sing songs with them and share Jesus with them. On our way back home from the orphanage, our youth pastor would stop at a local marketplace. He would split us into small groups, and we would have a couple hours to go eat and shop before we crossed back over the United States' border. On this particular month, after we'd left the orphanage, my youth pastor took us to the marketplace. After pairing me up with my group, we were given a time to return back to the youth van. I remember that I had a hard time keeping up with my group. They were a few years older than me and I knew they weren't too thrilled about having a little kid tagging along with them. We went into a few different shops and looked around. One shop in particular had some souvenirs I wanted to buy. I told the others in my group that I was going to pay for my items and that I'd be right back. When I finished paying, I returned to the spot where I left them, but they were not there. I called out their names, but I didn't see anyone from my group amongst the crowd. I began to feel myself panic as I tried to backtrack my steps from earlier. I returned to two of the stores we had shopped in. That's when I remembered a third store we had gone to. One of the youth in my group mentioned that she wanted to stop by that particular store before we left the marketplace to purchase something. I raced to find the store, but they all looked the same. I eventually found the exact store. I knew it was the store because when I walked in, I recognized the man working the register from earlier. He saw that I was panicked and told me to calm down. He then asked me (in Spanish) if he could help me. I told him in my very broken Spanish that I couldn't find my friends and asked him if he had seen the kids that I was in his shop with earlier. To my relief, he told me that they were there. He motioned to the back of the store and told me to follow the walkway around to the other side of the store. He said that's where they were shopping. I rushed to the back of the store and right as I turned the corner, I felt the man grab me from behind and drag me into a bathroom. I screamed and struggled to get away, but his grip on me was too tight. I remember struggling until I was exhausted. After that, I gave up. He raped me in that dark bathroom in the back of his store. I remember looking down at empty coke bottles on the ground and trying to process what was going on. I knew very little about sex. I was a virgin, but I did know that what the man was doing to me was wrong because everything on the inside of me was crying out. I had never been so afraid in my life; I had never felt so robbed in my life. When he was finished, I had no clue how long I had been in there; it felt like an eternity. He turned away from me to open the door and as soon as I saw the light of day come through, I ran. I ran as fast as I could. I felt filthier and dirtier than the trash that lined the streets I was running on. Tears streamed down my face uncontrollably. My thoughts raced and I kept asking myself if that monster had really just done what I thought he'd done. So many questions bombarded my mind. Suddenly, I spotted the youth group van on the other side of the street. The only problem was that it was across five lanes of busy traffic. Without even thinking, I ran across all five lanes of traffic. The horns blew and I almost got hit by one car and almost caused an accident with two other cars. I didn't care; I just kept running towards safety.

As I approached the van, everyone was in a frenzy, telling me that they had been searching for me. My youth pastor was scolding me for getting separated, while the group I had been with was asking me why I had strayed off. I kept trying to talk but no one was listening. I grabbed one of the girls from my youth group by the arm and frantically asked her to come with me to the bathroom. At the time, I wasn't sure what I planned to say to her. I just knew that I was in shock, afraid, and didn't quite know how to explain to my male youth pastor what had just happened. I wasn't even sure myself what had exactly happened. I remember feeling a lot of confusion, embarrassment and shame. As soon as I was safely inside the bathroom, I shut the stall door behind me. I remember pulling my panties down and seeing blood stains on them. My head began to spin and I almost passed out. I began to sob uncontrollably. *Oh God, please not that! No please; this can't be happening!* Those words screamed inside my head as the hot tears ran down my face. The feeling that I felt at the moment was one of such emptiness and brokenness. I had been robbed of my very innocence. The very thing I treasured and promised to my Savior that I would keep for my future husband was taken away from me like a thief snatches a wallet at gunpoint. The girl from the youth group heard me crying and knocked on the stall's door. "Are you okay? Is everything alright?" *No, everything wasn't alright,* I thought. I wasn't alright. I sat there on the toilet seat for a moment, feeling

numb and cold, but I managed to mutter the
words, "I'll be right out." I got myself together
and decided that I was way too ashamed to tell
her what had happened. I decided that I had to
tell my youth pastor. I remember thinking that although it would be hard to tell him, I had to do it.
He would protect me and he would make sure
that the person responsible would be punished.
We returned to the youth group van and my
youth pastor told everyone to load up. After everyone was loaded in the van, I stayed outside
and asked him if I could talk to him before we
took off. He reminded me that we were way behind schedule and the traffic would be a nightmare all the way back. Nevertheless, I told him it
was important and couldn't wait. So he told everyone in the van to stay put and we walked a little ways from the back of the van. That's when I
told him what happened to me to the best of my
ability. He didn't say anything the entire time I
was talking and when I finished, he remained
silent. I asked him if he heard what I said and he
responded that he had heard everything. The
words that followed were words that would
haunt me for many years after that day. He said,

"Cynthia, do you know how difficult it is to get permission to come down to Mexico and to come and help out the children in those orphanages?" I was confused at his line of questioning, nevertheless, I answered him, "No, I don't." He proceeded to explain to me that if anyone were to find out what had happened to me that day, our church would be in a lot of trouble. He went on to say that not only would our church be in a lot of trouble, the youth group would no longer be able to come to the orphanage anymore. According to him, all those children would be left without clothes, food, or be able to hear about Jesus. You cannot imagine the hurt that those words caused me. You can't begin to imagine the confusion I felt and the questions that ran through my mind. I tried to understand, but my mind could not grasp it.

I felt so powerless after the rape, but having a man who represented God to tell me to keep the entire thing a secret, hurt almost as much as the actual rape. He asked me if I understood what he was saying and I motioned my head in affirmation. I climbed in the back of the van and went to the furthest seat I could sit in. There, I curled up into a fetal position and silently cried the entire ride home. I was very sad. The spirit of rejection and other demonic spirits started rising up in me again. I felt ashamed, hurt and angry. Those haunting thoughts grew even more vicious. I heard, "You are so dirty now that you are disgusting to God. Where was God when you needed Him to protect you? He left you just like your father left you, your stepfather left you, and now, even your youth pastor has left you alone. God doesn't care about you. He let that man hurt you and now, God wants you to just take it. Just face it. You're nothing but damaged goods now. No man will ever want you. You're no good and you're nasty. You're nothing but a whore." As these words penetrated my mind, I didn't resist the thoughts or even cry out to God for help because honestly, I believed the lies of the enemy. I had tried my best to live a pure life and abstain from the things other girls my age were doing because I wanted to please and honor God, but it suddenly felt like it was all a waste. God didn't care about me. He took my stepdad and now, He'd let some strange man rape me. All I ever did was try to serve Him the best way I knew how. I remember deciding at that moment that God was just like every other man in my life. I agreed with the lies the devil whispered to me, and by doing so, I allowed the spirits of rejection, hurt, deep hurt, shame, and anger to come in and take root inside my soul. I felt anger surge over every part of my body and I felt the sensation of what felt to me like a heaviness suddenly come and rest on my shoulders. From that day forward, I was no longer the sweet, innocent young girl I once was. I was a broken, hurting, wounded soul and I hated myself with a passion. I trusted no one, especially God. What happened to me on this day was far more than just physical and emotional damage. It was a spiritual attack straight from hell.

I know now that I'd experienced a transference of demonic spirits from my rapist. Transference means to convey from one person, place, or situation to another; to cause to pass from one to another. Spirits can be transferred from one individual to another through the bloodline (inheritance), by association (soul ties), through the laying on of hands, and even without physical contact (i.e. psychic prayers, witchcraft, curses). El-isha received a double portion of Elijah's spirit (2 Kings 2:15) and Moses transferred the spirit of wisdom to Joshua through the laying on of hands (Deuteronomy 34:9) (John Eckhardt, Deliverance and Spiritual Warfare Manual/page 57).

As we see in these scriptures, good spirits such as an anointing and wisdom can be transferred, but so can evil spirits. The enemy will counterfeit or pervert things that God established for good to use for evil. In my case, this traumatic event was an open door that the enemy used to enter in by association (rape) and create a soul tie between me and my rapist. A soul tie is a joining of souls. This happens during sexual relations. It doesn't matter to the devil whether the sexual act was against a person's will or not. As I said earlier, the devil doesn't play fair. He is our enemy and he prowls around like a roaring lion looking for someone to devour (1 Peter 5:8). I began acting very differently in the months that followed the rape. I would isolate myself, experience bouts of rage and uncontrollable anger, and even become violent.

One day, my mom and I were arguing. She turned to walk down the flight of stairs and in a fit of rage, I came up behind her and pushed her. She fell down an entire flight of stairs. She was not hurt, but very shaken and she began to fear what I would do when we argued, so she would avoid getting me upset. I was out of control. I pulled away from my youth group, my church and God. I remember being physically present in the youth group and church, because my mom told me I had to be there, but my thoughts were far from God. I would have invasive thoughts that sounded like: "Why would I serve a God who allowed all this hurt in my life? God couldn't even protect me from harm." Because my youth pastor discouraged me from reporting the rape, I believed that he was a liar. In my teenage mind, he represented God to me, so I ultimately thought that God was a liar too. I was confused and angry and I began hanging out with the wrong type of crowd. I also became very promiscuous. The way I saw it, I was now damaged goods. There was no need for me to try to be a good girl anymore. No one was ever going to want me anyhow. I hurt so much that I would cry every night, trying to deal with the rape. I felt the most depressed on the nights when I would hear spirits whispering to me that I was disgusting to God. They told me that I was nothing but trash and the lowest of the low. I felt nasty and disgusting and the more I pushed those feelings down, the angrier I got.

My mom knew something wasn't right, even though she knew nothing about the rape. She would tell me constantly that she was praying for me and insisted that I attend the Christian school instead of the public school I was attending. She was constantly anointing my room, my bed and even my forehead with oil. She told everyone at church to pray for me.

One weekend, one of my friends and I were hanging out at a carnival and I met a much older man. We will call him Luis. Luis was 17 and I was 13. We started having a sexual relationship and we thought we were in love. My mom found out about Luis and forbade me to see him. Feeling like I couldn't live without Luis, I packed some belongings in a backpack and ran away with him. I was only gone two days before my family found me, but the fear that my running away put in my mom became a tool that I used to manipulate her whenever I wanted something. It wasn't long after I went home before I found out that Luis was living a double life. He lied to me, not only about his age (he was 23, not 17), but about his relationship status. It turned out that he was married with children. I totally flipped. I went to his job and spray painted profanity all over his car, plus, I broke out every one of his car's windows. I hated men and I hated God. Again the spirit of rejection, along with other demonic spirits, raged from within me. I was very angry, rebellious, hurt, bitter and prideful. I wanted to end my life. The only thing that eased my pain was attention from men, including negative attention.

I was done reaching out to my dad. At this point, he was living with his fiancé and they had their own new family. They didn't have time for a rebellious child like me. The summer before I was supposed to attend high school, my mom agreed to let me go to public school.

A few months before school began, my family

all went on a cruise together. On that cruise, I met a guy (we will call him Joe). Joe was significantly older than me; he was 23 and I was 14. After the cruise was over, we kept in touch. He lived in Georgia, but because he worked for an airline that allowed him to fly for free, he would come out to visit me in California. After we had been dating for a few months, he asked me to marry him. A few short months after that, we were married in Las Vegas. At the young age of 14, I was married and moving to Georgia, away from my mom and all the rest of my family. Although I was very young and had no business getting married, I wanted to get out of my hometown of Escondido. I wanted to escape the hurt and pain and I thought that leaving my home was the remedy. Looking back, I now know that me getting married at such a young age to a much older man was my attempt to fill an emptiness on the inside of me. That void had been caused by my father abandoning me, my stepfather's death and the rape. It was really a cry for help. I was hurting and broken and I wanted the pain to stop. I didn't want to get married; I wanted to be loved, but I was looking for love in all the wrong places and in all the wrong people. I needed a savior. I needed Jesus.

> *"He heals the brokenhearted*
> *and bandages their wounds."*
> Psalm 147:3 (ESV)

I needed Him to heal me, but the enemy and his demonic spirits had such a hold on me that I had given my will over to them. I was blinded by my pain and wanted nothing to with the Lord, but His love for me was unconditional.

So, as I settled into my new home in Georgia, I decided that since I was married and had a fresh new start in a new state that I would make the best of it. That's when my life got flipped upside down. Just five weeks after our wedding, my husband (Joe) and I had our first fight. Every couple has arguments now and then, but I learned on that day that the man Joe portrayed himself to be prior to the wedding was NOT who I was married to. During that argument, Joe raised his voice at me and shoved me. When I raised my voice back at him, he lifted me up and tossed me across the room like a rag doll. I jumped up in a rage and started swinging my fists at him. By the end of that argument, I had been punched, thrown and slapped until bruises covered most of my body. This type of abuse would be ongoing in our four-year marriage. It got so bad that the police would get tired of answering the domestic violence calls from our neighbors. Our fights were crazy. His rage and my rage seemed to ignite each other's rage. Again, this is an example of transference of spirits. Demonic spirits in one person can give strength to demons in another through transference (John Eckhardt, Deliverance and Spiritual Warfare Manual/page 58.)

I quickly found out where his rage came from. His father was very abusive to his mother and Joe had grown up witnessing domestic violence all throughout his childhood. On the other hand, I was full of anger from the hurts and trauma I had endured. Now, to add even more hurt and pain to my life, having the man I'd married beat me on a daily basis was just too much for me to bear. After six months of marriage, I suffered a terrible miscarriage. I lost so much blood that I had to be hospitalized. It was necessary for the doctors to perform what is called a D&C. Because of the abuse I suffered, the baby I was carrying had literally been beaten apart in me. While under anesthesia, the doctor saw the bruising that covered my body. When I returned to my hospital room from surgery, there was a social worker there, questioning me about my bruises. Being a typical battered woman, I lied and covered up for my husband. She pleaded with me to tell her the truth, reassuring me that she could keep me safe from my husband if he was the one who'd hurt me. Nevertheless, I was so codependent that I couldn't imagine my life without him, even though my life was chaotic and I was miserable. I was sure that he would stop beating me; he just needed another chance and for me to love him better. I remember the disappointment on her face when she realized that she wasn't going to convince me to give him up. After she left my hospital room, Joe came in, reached under the bed sheets, grabbed my arm tightly, pressed his face right up to my ear and said, "If you told that woman that I laid one finger on you, I swear when I get you home, I'm going to kill you." At that moment, I believed that he would. The spirit of fear gripped my very being and I would live in fear of him from that day on.

Later that night, my mom flew in from California. When she walked into my hospital room, I felt like I was safe again. I was so happy to see her. The following morning, I was released from the hospital. My mom and Joe took me into our small apartment and my mother went back outside to get the rest of the belongings from the car. While she was outside, my neighbor discretely came over to my mom and warned her to get me out of that house before Joe beat me to death. My mom had no clue what the neighbor was talking about. She came in and began to question Joe and before long, Joe was enraged an out of control. That's when my mom saw his wrath firsthand. After he calmed down, he immediately began to repent and promised, as he had done so many other times, that it would never happen again. My mom immediately went into her psychologist role. She made him swear not to ever put his hands on me again and told him that he needed professional help. She told us to find a counselor and start going to marriage counseling. She told him to get into some anger management classes and he promised her that he would. My mom asked me if he had been abusive to me prior to the beating that caused my miscarriage, but I lied to her and said that he had not. I told her that this was an isolated event. The truth is—he had been abusive to me many times.

Even though I was hurt and abused by Joe on a continuous basis, I did not want to leave him. I believed that I deserved to be treated the way he treated me. After all, I believed that I was worthless and I was lucky that he was even willing to put up with me. When he wasn't beating me, he was never affectionate or loving. If he acknowledged me in the slightest bit, I was thrilled. I settled for crumbs of attention, just like I had from my biological father. I remember being in the midst of the abuse and thinking that this type of treatment was the way a husband was supposed to treat his wife.

One day, I was so fed up with his abuse that I decided to tell his mom how he was treating me.

When I told her that her son had been beating me, she looked at me unfazed and said, "Honey, you better get used to it. His father did the same to me our entire marriage." So I began to think that this was how love worked. *Love hurts, right?* Every other man in my life who said he loved me had hurt me, so I reasoned with myself that love and hurt go hand in hand. My need to fill the emptiness grew more and more as I was broken down by words and repeated beatings by Joe. I needed him to love me, approve of me and do for me what every other man had not done. Instead, all I got was more pain, pain on top of pain, and hurt on top of hurt.

CHAPTER 5

A Baby Having Babies

Four months after the miscarriage, I found out I was pregnant again. It was bittersweet for me. I was thrilled to be having my first baby but, at the same time, I was afraid for my safety and the safety of my child. After telling Joe of the pregnancy, he went into a rage. He accused me of cheating and was adamant that he was not the father. He told me to pack all my clothes because he was kicking me out. He kept swearing at me and calling me every name a man should never call any woman, let alone his wife. As we drove out to the middle of nowhere, he reached over me and swung open the passenger's door. With a hard shove, he pushed me out of the car. He threw out my belongings as well. I thought I would die that night. All I remember thinking was, *Oh God, please keep my baby safe.* I lay on the side of that dirt road skinned up and down my body, quivering with fear. Suddenly, I heard the sound of a car radio coming closer to me. "Oh God; he's coming back!" I whispered. I thought for sure he was going to run me over to make sure I was dead. Just then, I heard a man's voice say, "Ma'am are you okay?" I couldn't see his face, but I trusted him. He helped me into his pick-up truck. That's when I heard Joe's voice screaming at the man. "Hey, that's my wife; you better take her out of that truck!" I'll never forget the sound I heard next. It was the sound of the man's shot-gun cocking loudly. I turned to see what was going on and watched as this man had the double barrel of a sawed-off shot gun pointed right at Joe. "You better get back in your car boy and drive away and I'll pretend like I never saw you. Either that or we can handle it a different way; it's your choice," said the Good Samaritan. Joe shouted out a few words of profanity at him and then got in his car and drove away. A part of me wished that the man had shot him dead that night. I really felt that death was the only way I would get free from his abuse. The Good Samaritan got back into the truck and told me not to worry; he was going to take me straight to the hospital. He stayed with me until they contacted my mom. I was admitted to the hospital under strict supervision. My mom flew in from California that next morning. I moved back to California with just the clothes on my back. I stayed there until after the birth of my first son, Anthony. He was absolutely perfect. I had been estranged for most of my pregnancy from Joe. My mom encouraged me to get a divorce and leave him for good, but I still wanted to believe that he would somehow change, especially now that he was a father. My mother begged me not to move back to Georgia, but when Anthony was six months old, I took a cab to the airport. I left without even saying goodbye to my mom. I moved back to Georgia and back into the hands of my abuser.

Within weeks of moving back, the abuse started up again. Three months later, I found out I was pregnant again. My mom ended up selling her house in California and moving to Georgia to be close to me; she wanted to make sure that I was safe. She told me that she was so worried for my safety that she couldn't sleep at night when she was living in California. The stress had caused her to suffer from insomnia.

The violence would escalate even more during my pregnancies, so like I had with my first pregnancy, I lived with my mom while pregnant with my second son, Andrew. Joe would get so jealous of the baby I was carrying that he would intentionally try to punch me in the stomach. Out of fear that I would miscarry again, I moved back in with my mom. I'm sure my mom was certain that I would leave Joe this time, but no such luck. Just like before, after Andrew was born, Joe came around saying all the right things. He said everything I wanted to hear and I moved back in with him. This time, my aunt Norma and her husband moved in with us as well. This was a huge help to me. My aunt was like a second mother to me. I became very close to her. She saw firsthand the abuse I would suffer, but she never judged me; she would just encourage me. I thought that them living with us would stop Joe from being so crazy and violent, but that wasn't the case. As a matter of fact, it only seemed to get worse. My family would try to intervene and protect me, so it became a family riot. No family in their right mind will allow someone to beat up a member of their family. After a while, the fighting was just too much. Joe kicked them out for the last time and they left. After they left, things got worse. Joe would "punish" me for not "obeying him" by taking the kids from me. He would take them to his mom's house and leave me alone at the house. I would be stuck there. I had no car and had never learned to drive. Afraid and ashamed to tell my mother that the abuse was still going on, I would hide from her because I was tired of making up lies about black eyes and bruises. My pain began to override my fear. I started to devise a plan of escape in my head. I walked to a local grocery store and applied for a job. I began working and saving my money, with the intentions of leaving the monster I was married to. I figured that after a few paychecks, I'd have enough money to get my own place. Nevertheless, shortly after I got the job, we had another fight and I endured another beating, but this time, he targeted my oldest son, Anthony. Anthony was one and a half years old. I had just put him in his baby bath seat and sat him in the bathtub. Joe came in and began shouting at me. The baby began to cry when hearing Joe's raised tone. He yelled at the baby to shut up and when I told him not to talk to him that way, he slapped me across my face. Anthony began screaming as Joe continued to hit me. When Anthony's cries got louder, Joe walked over to the tub and slapped Anthony across the face so hard that his little body came out the side of the bath seat and he went under the water. I rushed to grab him and I retrieved him from under the water. I held him in my arms as I comforted his shaking body. At that moment, something in me clicked; it was just like a light switch. I calmly apologized to Joe for making him angry and asked him to forgive me. I proceeded to dry Anthony off and get him dressed, all the while, acting as if everything was completely fine. I watched as Joe began to pack his gym bag to go play basketball. I asked him what time he would be back. He didn't respond; he just slammed the door behind himself as he left. I waited until I heard his car leave and then, I called my mom and asked her to come get the babies. I'll never forget the look on her face when I opened the door to greet her. I hadn't seen her in a few days because I had a black eye and scratches on my neck. She began to cry. I told her there was no time for that. I explained to her that I was leaving Joe, this time for good. Whether she believed me or not, like always, she supported me. We moved quickly to get the kids in her car and once I knew the kids were safely in her care, I did something I hadn't done in a long time. I prayed. I still remember my prayer that day. I told God that I was very afraid and I needed His help. I explained to Him that if I left Joe, I was going to be a single mom and all alone. I was 17 years old with two children, no car and a minimum wage job that paid me four dollars an hour. I told Him all my fears and asked Him to please give me strength this time to leave for good. After I was done praying, I walked over to the house phone and dialed 911. The police came and I reported all of the abuse and how he had struck my child. Within an hour, they had arrested Joe and were taking him into custody. The police told me that I should get into a battered women's shelter to ensure that my kids and I would be safe if and when Joe bailed out of jail. The thought of him coming after me or my family gripped me with fear. My mom decided that she would stay with a friend in a secure location in case he came looking for the kids at her house. I called a friend of mine I had met while working at the grocery store (we will call him Matt). Matt knew about my situation and had encouraged me to get out, but like everyone else, he couldn't convince me either. He came and picked me and the kids up that night and took us to the store. He bought formula and diapers for my sons and paid for us to stay in a hotel for the night. The next morning, my children and I went to the shelter. They helped me to get a lawyer and within six months, I was divorced from Joe and pregnant by Matt. I was pregnant with my third son, Julian.

CHAPTER 6

Broken But Still Alive

Like any broken, co-dependent woman, I jumped into a relationship before I could even begin to heal from the trauma of the relationship I had just come out of, but we didn't care. Matt and I were in love and wanted to spend the rest of our lives together. Matt loved my two sons like they were his own. He showered me and them with love. Matt treated me like a queen. We were both eighteen years old and so broke that we could hardly make ends meet, but we were happy. We began attending church together.

One Sunday morning, Matt answered the altar call and committed his life to Christ. I rededicated mine that day and the Lord began to work in our lives. We wanted to do things right in the eyes of God and desired His blessings on our relationship, so two months before Julian was born,

Matt and I got married. Life was good, but time does not heal all wounds. I had a very hard time trusting Matt. For a long time, I expected Matt to stop the nice guy facade and start abusing me like my ex-husband had done. I also had a hard time differentiating what things had taken place with Joe versus what had taken place with Matt. I would accuse him at times of doing things or saying things that he had never done or said. Plus, I had some huge self-esteem issues and I wasn't used to having a peaceful life, so I would pick arguments with Matt, because fighting and arguing was what I was used to. This was not the healthiest way to begin a marriage, but I tried to warn Matt of that before we got married. I told him, in so many words, to run for his life because I was a mess. He refused to leave me and told me that he wanted to raise our son together. He said that he wanted to raise Anthony and Andrew as his own and eventually, I agreed to let him.

After Matt lost his job at the factory, he found another job at a seafood market. I gave birth to Julian and shortly after, we decided to pack up our family and move back to California. We wanted to begin a new life in a new state and leave all our problems behind in Georgia. Somehow, those problems seemed to jump in the moving van with us because when we got to California, all my pain and unresolved hurt from my first marriage and my past was still right there with me. I began attending adult school to help me prepare to get my GED, since I had never completed high school. I dropped out my freshman year to get married.

While I was attending night school, I met a girl who was my age (we will call her Sarah). Sarah had a son about the same age as my three-year-old son, Anthony. I hadn't had friends since I left school. My first husband was too jealous and controlling to allow me to have friends, so I liked having a girlfriend that I could hang out with. We would study together while the kids played to-gether and entertained themselves. Around that same time, Matt taught me how to drive. I felt pretty independent once I was driving and work-ing towards my GED. This made me feel quite productive.

One day, while I was at Sarah's house hanging

out, she pulled out a small bag of what looked to me like white little rocks. She asked me if I had ever tried Meth before. I told her no. I had never tried it nor had I ever heard of it. She took out one of the small rocks and set it on top of a mirror. She reached into her purse and pulled out a credit card and began crushing the rock until it was a fine powder. After that, she separated it into two equal lines, rolled up a dollar bill into a straw, and snorted one of the lines up her nose. She handed me the dollar bill and said, "Here. You try it." I hesitated for a moment. She then said, "Stop being so scary; just try it. I promise you will love it." I took the dollar bill and mimicked what I'd seen her do. I hadn't even snorted half the line when a euphoric rush came over my entire body. Every insecurity, fear, and worry was suddenly gone. I felt carefree and on top of the world. Sarah and Meth became my newfound friends. I would hang out with her almost every day and sometimes even spend the night at her house. Meth would make me super paranoid, so I always worried that my husband would find out what I was doing. Another side effect of Meth was weight loss. I had been heavy most of my life and literally in a matter of a month, I dropped about thirty pounds. Oh how I loved the new-found attention I received from men.

One night, while hanging out at Sarah's house, some of her guy friends brought over more Meth for us. After we had all partaken of it, Sarah and the other guy disappeared into her bedroom, leaving me and his friend alone in the living room. The guy began to touch and grab me, so I explained to him that I was married. He didn't seem to care and told me that I couldn't have expected him and his friend just to share their drugs with us and not expect anything in return. His tone scared me and I remember feeling like I was backed into a corner. I was so mad at Sarah for putting me in that position. We had sex and after he was done, I felt horrible. All I could think of was how nasty and disgusting I was. I didn't know why I had cheated on my husband. The guilt began to eat me up. The more guilt I felt, the more Meth I did.

One night, it all fell apart and I had an experience that changed my life. I was wide awake and

had been up for a few days. I was in my bedroom
and Matt was asleep. I remember this overwhelming feeling of sadness coming over me. I
began to cry uncontrollably. I went into the bathroom to wash my face and when I looked in the
mirror, I couldn't stand what I saw. I searched in
the medicine cabinet for my stash of Meth, but
when I found it, instead of using it to get high, I
flushed it down the toilet. I began to cry again
uncontrollably and look for pills in the medicine
cabinet that I could take. When I couldn't find
any, I went to the kitchen and grabbed a knife. I
tried for about ten minutes to slit my wrist, but I
was too scared to do it. Just then, I heard voices
in my head, telling me that my life was worthless.
I was a cheating whore, a terrible drug addict,
and a horrible mom. The demonic spirit of death
encouraged me to kill myself, saying that my family was better off with me dead anyway. As I ran
the knife over the veins on the inside of my wrist,
I just couldn't bring myself to do it. That's when I
reached for the phone book and called a suicide
hotline. The lady on the other line was trying her
best to understand me, but I was hysterical.
About this time, Matt had awakened because he'd

heard the sound of me crying. I hung up the phone with the woman from the suicide hotline because the voices I heard in my head were louder than the lady on the other line. I remember screaming for all the voices to shut up, but they didn't. They just kept on saying horrible things about me that I felt were all true. I didn't know what to do, so I began to say "Jesus, Jesus, Jesus." I said it over and over until the voices stopped and there was nothing but silence. That's when I felt a warmth come over my entire body. I heard a soft voice say to me "You're safe now. I'm with you and I'll never leave you. Rest now." The comfort I felt from this voice calmed everything in me. I fell asleep and the next morning, I awoke a brand new person. I stopped using Meth with no problem. I just quit cold turkey.

I tried to tell Sarah about my experience and how I believed the devil was trying to convince me to end my life. I told her that God had intervened and saved my life. I begged her to quit using Meth too, but she told me that she would never quit. She then told me to leave her house talking all that "God stuff." I left that day and the last time I heard about her, she was homeless and had lost custody of her son. I took a long hard look at my life. It had been just three months from the time I met Sarah and started doing Meth until the day it ended, but the entire thing had frightened me. I began to realize that the pain I had from the things I'd endured in my past weren't just magically going to go away. I needed to deal with them, but I had no clue how to do that. In my efforts to try to find the answer, I looked to God.

CHAPTER 7

The Ministry

Matt was attending a church that we found in Hemet, California, the new city we lived in. I joined him in attendance as well. We thrived at this new church. The congregation was so accepting and loving towards us and our children. After a few months, we began to serve in the children's ministry and my husband became an usher. After we had proven ourselves faithful in those positions, we were asked to lead the children's ministry. We were thrilled to have the opportunity to serve as leaders in the church. We began to grow in the knowledge of the Lord and become strong in our faith. My husband served as our pastor's armor bearer and began to travel with him to different churches.

One Sunday after service, our pastor asked us to have a meeting with him. He began to explain to us that the Lord had a call on our lives. He went on to say that God had shown him that we were called to pastor a church he was going to be opening up. He told us that he wanted us to complete the requirements to be ordained and once we had done that, he would ordain and help us get into a church building. We would have our own church. Matt and I were overwhelmed with joy. This was a confirmation of the things the Lord had already put in our heart. Shortly after that meeting, we completed the ordination requirements. At the young age of 21, Matt and I were ordained into the ministry as Pastors and we began pastoring a church in Banning, California in 2007.

Being pastors while working secular jobs as well as raising three boys was quite a job, but we managed. We struggled at times with our finances. We lived paycheck to paycheck, but we loved the work of the ministry and we did it unto the Lord. God always met our needs and provided for us. Being that we came from a "Word of Faith" ministry, we were taught to be givers. Our pastors taught us so much about giving, healing, miracles and faith. That firm foundation was ingrained in us and I am grateful to this day that it was.

I can remember being in my twenties, sitting among ministers much older than us and way more seasoned in the faith. We would be at ministerial conferences with some of the great pioneers of faith like Brother Kenneth Hagin and Kenneth Copeland. I would sit in awe, just taking it all in. The anointing on these men of God's lives blew me away. The miracles and testimonies that we witnessed in those meetings coupled with the power of God that was tangible in the atmosphere was like nothing I had ever experienced. Howbeit, even being around great people of faith and witnessing miracles did not mean my faith was great. In all honesty, I had deep trust issues concerning the Lord. Yes, I had grown so much in the Lord. I had grown in my faith. I would even go so far as to say that my faith was strong, but I had conditions and limitations on my heart concerning my relationship with my heavenly Father. God knew it and I knew it. I didn't look broken on the outside any longer, but on the inside, I was a mess. Yes, I had graduated from Bible College, was leading praise and worship in our church, and preaching at least once a month in our women's ministry, but I knew and God knew that I hadn't completely surrendered my life to Him because I didn't trust Him fully. I trusted Him more than I'd trusted Him in the past, but I didn't completely trust Him with my life. I knew this because of my fruit. Fear was a big issue for me. I was a giver, but I was always afraid to give. It was a lot easier for Matt to give, but for me, it was tough. In the back of my mind, I would always think, "Okay, maybe this is going to be the time that God is going to let me down." I was also in denial about a lot of the things I had endured in my past. I didn't want to think about my father, the rape or even begin to deal with the abuse from my first marriage. I honestly wanted to be free and desired to have a relationship with the Lord that had no limitations. This also spilled over into my marriage. I had deep intimacy issues. I didn't enjoy sex or intimacy. I also had huge issues with my body and self-image. Yes, I was a mess, but I could preach fire about healing and wholeness to other women, however, I had no clue how to receive it and apply to my own life. Another battle for me was my mind. I was always worried about what people would think of me. I also felt that as the "First Lady" in the church, I couldn't tell anyone I was feeling this way or talk about the issues and the struggles I faced in my marriage either. After all, what would they think of me? As the pastor's wife, I'm supposed to know better. I'm supposed to have a handle on my own life, right? I'm supposed to know and be an expert on how to deal with all types of issues. My life should be one that exemplified a woman who had forgiven everyone who'd ever wronged her, a woman who had it all together, correct? WRONG! Nothing was further from the truth. I have since learned that these are lies that the enemy tells people who are in ministry so they will feel shame and guilt about their own struggles. The devil will condemn a person in ministry until they are under so much condemnation that they feel they cannot reach out to anyone. This causes them to isolate themselves and keep their issues hidden, but the Lord doesn't desire for any of our issues to be hidden or tucked away. He wants to expose the enemy and bring those deep-rooted issues to light so He can heal our brokenness.

> *"The LORD is near to the brokenhearted, and*
> *saves those who are crushed in spirit."*
> *Psalm 34:18 (NIV)*

I looked the part, but instead of dealing with my issues, I would slap a big Band-Aid on my hurt and make a vague statement like, "Well, it's all under the blood." I would pretend like I wasn't still that scared, hurt little girl who was still angry at all the men who'd hurt her. I was so bound by my hurts and fears that I lived my life looking through a veil of hurt. Pain dimmed my vision and I needed deliverance. Nevertheless, I knew nothing about deliverance. I knew about prosperity, faith and healing, but deliverance was not spoken of. To my knowledge, deliverance was not being taught in word of faith circles. The very thing that I so desperately needed was a part of my covenant as a child of God and yet, I was not aware of it.

> *"My people are destroyed because they lack*

knowledge of me."
Hosea 4:6 (ISV)

The enemy will meet us at our point of ignorance. Such was the case for me. Deliverance is the children's bread (Mark 7:27) and a part of my covenant with God, but because I didn't know it was available to me and I lacked knowledge regarding deliverance, the enemy went unexposed in my life. This was destroying me one day at a time, causing me great pain in my life.

CHAPTER 8

The Thief Returns

In our sixth year of marriage, I found out I was pregnant with my daughter, Elizabeth. I was sure the baby would be another boy, making it my fourth son, but I was shocked when the sonogram showed that I was having a girl. Life seemed complete now with a daughter to add to our family and for a while, things in our marriage seemed to get better. We continued to pastor, but we relocated the church in Banning, California to the city we lived in: Hemet, California. The church began to grow and we had a nice congregation of families to lead. As far as our home life and our marriage, things were fine. We would have our occasional arguments, but overall, it seemed like we had grown in our relationship and gotten past many of our biggest issues.

My husband and I decided that for our ten

year anniversary, we would renew our wedding vows on a cruise ship and have our family and church family join in our celebration. Our spiritual parents cruised with us too and performed the ceremony on board. It was a beautiful ceremony and Matt surprised me with a beautiful new wedding ring set. It was a wonderful anniversary. From the outward appearance, it appeared that we were the perfect family, but as quickly as we'd disembarked the ship, our marriage was under attack again. Those spirits of rejection, hurt, and pain that were just under the surface of my heart began to show their ugly heads. We started struggling in our marriage. Most of the struggle stemmed from my past hurts, but my husband had endured his own childhood hurts as well. He also had a spirit of rejection from growing up with an alcoholic mother. Additionally, he'd been molested as a young child by family members outside the home. This is where the spirit of rejection entered into him and took root. All of these unresolved issues with demons and roots caused much hurt and many arguments in our marriage. We were like puppets on a string and the devil was the puppeteer, manipulating us as he pleased. My intimacy issues continued and the spirit of shame and self-rejection in me played off the spirit of rejection in him. We went to marriage counseling and talked, argued, cried, and prayed, but we both desperately needed deliverance.

"When evening had come, they brought to Him many who were demon-possessed. And He cast out the spirits with a word, and healed all who were sick."
Matthew 8:16 (NAS 1977)

Notice that the scripture says Jesus cast out the spirits. Demons cannot be counseled out, talked out, fought out, or prayed out; they must be CAST OUT! I honestly didn't know that the answer was deliverance and neither did my husband. Yes, we were in ministry and we had seen demons cast out of people before, but they were unbelievers or people like the man on the street corner who reeked of alcohol and talked to himself. Of course, they had demons because they weren't saved. I was saved, sanctified, and filled with the Holy Ghost, so there was no way in the world a demon was living in me or my husband.

The first time I watched the movie *Poltergeist*, I was so scared that I couldn't sleep for a week. I remember my mom telling me to simply plead the blood over myself because only unbelievers could be possessed, not Christians. This is one of the traditional beliefs that are passed down and you just believe it because your family was always taught that. Even while in Bible College, this same belief was confirmed. Christians cannot have an evil spirit living in them because the Holy Spirit could not live inside the same body in which demons abode. Christians, however, could be oppressed, regressed, digressed, obsessed and suppressed, but never possessed. We believed that a demon could be *outside* a Christian oppressing him, but that it could not be *inside* him (John Eckhardt, Can a Christian Have a Demon?/ *Charisma News*. N.p., 29 Aug. 2015). I have since learned that this too is another great ploy and deception of the enemy. A Christian can have a demon or, in my case, many demons and the only way to get them out is by receiving deliverance. It is true that a demon cannot "possess" a believer's spirit, but we are not just spirit beings, we are three part beings. John Eckhardt goes on to explain it this way: Every person is made up of three parts: spirit, soul and body. When Jesus comes into a believer's life, He comes into that person's spirit. John 3:6 tells us clearly, "That which is born of the Spirit is spirit" (NKJV). A demon cannot dwell in a Christian's spirit because that is where Jesus and the Holy Spirit dwells. It is the other components that make up a human being—the soul (mind, will and emotions) and the body—that are the targets of demonic attack. Demons can dwell in those areas of a Christian's life. So when we say that a Christian is demonized or possessed, we are not saying he has a demon in his spirit, but in some part of his soul or body (John Eckhardt, Can a Christian Have a Demon?"/ *Charisma News*. N.p., 29 Aug. 2015). No matter how much my husband and I tried to put the Lord in the center of our marriage, all of our deep-rooted spirits pushed God right on out. This was not the plan of God for our marriage. God wants His fruit of the Spirit abounding in every marriage. He desires that our marriages be full of life and life more abundantly.

God loves the union of marriage. He created it and ordained it.

"For this reason a man will leave his father and mother and be united to his wife, and the two will become one flesh.' So they are no longer two, but one flesh."
Mark 10:7-8 (NIV)

Our marriage was not the picture of a God-or- dained marriage because, even though we loved God and served Him in ministry, two broken peo- ple do not make a whole. I kept on looking to my husband to be my rescuer and in doing so, prove to me that he wasn't going to let me down or abandon me like every other man in my life. So every time he "fell short" in my eyes, I was devas- tated. I would then lash out at him because I felt let down and this would just solidify that spirit of rejection in him; this was a vicious cycle that my husband and I were stuck in. I had put impossi- ble expectations on a mere man that only God could completely fulfill.

"Be strong and of a good courage, fear not, nor be

afraid of them: for the LORD thy God, he it is that doth go with thee; he will not fail thee, nor forsake thee."
Deuteronomy 31:6 (KJV)

"Jesus looked at them and said, "With man this is impossible, but not with God; all things are possible with God."
Mark 10:17 (NIV)

The attack on our marriage progressively got worse. My husband lost his secular job and we began to struggle financially. We got behind on our bills and before long, the repo man was showing up at our home to take my car and some of the furniture from our home. The landlord was on our backs and the utilities were being shut off. The arguing continued and even grew worst. Our sons started acting out in school because of the chaos in our home. The more we tried to hold things together, the faster they crumbled. Before long, the church's congregation began to dwindle down. I began to resent the church because there were fewer people, which meant less giving. This meant we would have to foot the costs of the church's bills, along with our own bills. The pressure and stress in our home could be cut with a knife. When we could no longer carry the church's bills, we had to close the church.

The day we closed the church down was one of the saddest days of my life. Once those doors were closed and we walked away from that call, things went from bad to worst. I thought we would have a bit of relief with the financial burden of the church off of us, but that was not the case. All hell broke loose in our home. My husband and I were living like roommates. There was no intimacy or communication between us and sex was the last thing on my mind. I was too stressed; I worried about the bills and keeping a roof over our heads to even think about any type of intimacy. My husband was able to get a job in his field for significantly less than what he had been making at his previous job, but we were just happy that he'd found work. Our marriage was barely holding on by a thread, but my shame and pride were overshadowed by the fear of losing my marriage. Because of this, I reached out to a few of my sisters-in-Christ. These were other ministers' wives that I had gotten to know over the course of our years in ministry. When I told them that we had closed the church and were struggling in our marriage, they cut me off like the plague. They acted like a "bad marriage" was contagious. They completely turned their backs on me and this only broke me all the more. The spirit of rejection was in full swing and it was being stirred up in me again. I felt rejected, hurt, let down, abandoned and I was incredibly angry. Again, I was looking to man to do for me what only God could do. I kept expecting a man to save me, but one already had. Jesus was my rescuer and the only savior I needed, but I just couldn't get my eyes off man. The last rejection brought up the spirit of "church hurt" again. I remember relating in my mind how my youth pastor had let me down after my rape and in my eyes, had turned his back on me when I needed him the most. These feelings led to hatred in my heart for the things of God. I felt I had done things right in the eyes of God, but He'd failed me because of the way my life was going. The enemy knew this too because I was constantly speaking death over my marriage and my fruit showed the bitterness that lived in my heart. Again, the enemy never missed an opportunity to pay me a visit. He would use my own wicked and hidden desires to further lure me away from the plan of God for my life. He used this to bring destruction to my household and I would willingly go because my hurt and shame had turned my heart cold towards the Lord.

One day, while picking up my daughter from school, a few of the moms befriended me and asked me to lunch. While at lunch and after a few glasses of wine, I opened up to them about my problems. They told me everything I wanted to hear; they told me how wrongly I was being treated and how my husband didn't deserve me. They invited me to go out with them that weekend and get away for some "me time" to get my mind off of all my worries. Everything in me told me not to go with them, but a part of me was curious. I told myself that there was nothing wrong with having some fun with the girls and going out for a night on the town. I should have run in the opposite direction, but instead, I walked toward the path of destruction as a sheep being led to the slaughter.

"Enter not into the path of the wicked, and go not in the way of evil men. Avoid it, pass not by it, turn from it, and pass away. For they sleep not, except they have done mischief; and their sleep is taken away, unless they cause some to fall."
Proverbs 4:14-16 (KJV)

That weekend, the girls and I went to a night-club. I had never been in a nightclub. They all went up to the bar and ordered drinks. I walked up to the bar with them, having no clue what to order. I could count on two hands how many times I had drunk alcohol in my life. A man at the end of the bar sent over a drink to me and I thanked him with a smile. I then made my way back to the table where my newfound friends were sitting. They seemed to know everyone who was anyone in the club. I felt like I was see-ing a part of the world I had never seen before and honestly, I was infatuated with the whole scene. I had been a married woman and a mom for what seemed to be my entire life. This scene was all new to me. After sipping my drink a few times, I began to feel my head spinning. I followed the girls out onto the dance floor and we danced the night away. I enjoyed the attention I received from men. I kept reassuring myself that I wasn't doing anything wrong; it was just a little flirting, but it was all harmless. I remember coming home that night past midnight. My husband was already asleep and I slipped into bed without waking him up.

The next morning, he asked me what time I had come in and he questioned me about my new friends. I resented the fact that he was treating me like I couldn't be trusted. I knew that he didn't like the idea that I was out so late, but I didn't care. I had a spirit of rebellion that had rooted itself in me a long time ago and it was now seeing its opportunity to rise up. At that moment, I decided that I didn't care whether he liked that I was going out or not. I enjoyed it and I was a grown woman, so I could do as I pleased. Anyhow, I felt that he didn't have any right to tell me where to go or what to do; he couldn't even take care of the bills in his own house. This decision began a whirlwind of events. I began going out with the girls almost every weekend—partying, drinking and dancing. I convinced myself that because I wasn't going home with any of the men I was dancing and flirting with at the club that I wasn't doing anything wrong. The women I was hanging out with also introduced me to marijuana. I also began smoking Black-n-Mild's to look "sophisticated" at the club. At this point, I had stopped attending church altogether because I was usually returning home from the club at two o'clock on Sunday mornings. My kids noticed a huge change in me as well. They were used to me being up bright and early on the weekends, making big Saturday morning meals or preparing supper for after church, not hungover in bed until noon. My husband was left to watch all the kids as I went out until the wee hours of the morning, but I wasn't the only one the enemy was working on. While I was out on the town, my husband was confiding in a female co-worker about our marital problems and she was happy to console him. When I found out about this innocent little "friendship," I went ballistic. My husband assured me that nothing happened; he then told me that I was acting irrational and questioned me about how far I had gone while out at my frequent nightclub outings. This caused a huge argument. I remember we didn't speak for a couple days.

It was becoming increasingly obvious that our marriage was slipping through our fingers, but we had no clue what we should do about it. Out of fear of losing what little bit of a marriage we had left, he decided to quit his job to assure me that my beliefs that he was having an affair with this co-worker were false. When I found out that he'd quit his job, I was furious. One of the main issues I had in our relationship was trust. I never felt that I could trust him to financially meet the needs of our family and this was the last and final straw for me. My friends had been sowing seeds in me about leaving him, so the idea had been lingering in my mind for some time and was about to come to pass. I gathered up the kids and we went and stayed at a girlfriend's home. As I talked to her that night, she fed my fears and confirmed all my doubts. She told me that I should move out and separate from my husband. She convinced me that doing so would cause him

to "wake up" and start doing a better job at pro-
viding for me and I foolishly listened to her.

"Fools find no pleasure in understanding but de-
light in airing their own opinions."
Proverbs 18:2 (NIV)

I knew better than to take advice about my
marriage from a non-believer, but my hurt overrode my beliefs. It was at this point in my life that
the spirit of rebellion was in full operation within
me. I knew that I had two options. I could forget
about everyone turning their backs on me when I
went to them for godly advice. I could decide that
I had all of Heaven backing me up and I had the
authority to come against every assignment of
hell against my marriage. I could have believed
God for my marriage and I could have chosen to
fight for my marriage, but I didn't. Deep down in
me, that spirit of rebellion was stirred up. I liked
my newfound freedom and my new party lifestyle. Yes, we had issues in our marriage that
needed to be worked out, but I didn't care anymore. As a matter of fact, being married, in some
ways, cramped my new lifestyle of freedom. My

grandmother used to have a saying and it went: "Tell me who your friends are and I'll tell you who you are." Now, I'm not in any way blaming the company of friends that I kept back then for my wrong decisions. I take full responsibility for my choices, but they were definitely a voice of negativity speaking into my life and I listened to every word they said.

"Blessed is the man that walked not in the counsel of the ungodly, nor standeth in the way of sinners, nor sitteth in the seat of the scornful."
Psalm 1:1 (KJV)

I made the decision to move out. I found a small apartment in the city I lived in and told my husband I was leaving him. He was shocked. It was one of the many sad days to follow in our home.

CHAPTER 9

Rejecting the Call

The next few months were horrible. I was so different. It was like I was a completely different person. The spirit of rejection, along with its buddies: hurt, rebellion, lust and many others ran rampart in me. I was partying all the time and my outward image began to match what was going on inside me. There is one day in particular that stands out in my mind the most. I had always desired to get my lip pierced, but never did it because I had been too concerned about what others would say about me. I knew then that rebellion was in my heart, but now, I had an excuse to let it loose. As I said at the beginning, those tares that had been sown in me from my early childhood had sprung up. They were now fully grown and becoming exposed in and through my actions.

"You can identify them by their fruit, that is, by the way they act."
Matthew 7:16 (NLT)

I remember driving to the tattoo shop and sensing that my decision to get my first piercing was very grieving to the spirit of God. I intentionally pushed aside the apprehension I felt. I remembered all the good I believed I had done for the Lord and that's when I felt anger rising up in me for the way my life had turned out. I no longer needed a God who allowed me to go through so much pain. I declared something into the atmosphere that day that I will never forget. As I parked the car in the parking lot, I felt empowered and free to do what I chose to do when I chose to do it. I slammed my car door with pride and as I walked into the tattoo parlor, I said to the Lord (please excuse my vulgarity), "Lord, this is my middle finger to you." That was my way of saying, "Middle finger to your ways, your ministry, and your call on my life." In other words, I was divorcing myself, not only from my husband, but from the Lord. This was harsh, but in my heart, that's exactly how I felt. Every time I got another tattoo or piercing after that point in my life, I was reaffirming that declaration all over again. Please hear me, I am not saying that piercings and tattoos are wrong for everybody, but for me, my piercings and tattoos were an outward statement of my rebellion. It was a clear demonstration of the prideful heart and arrogant demeanor that I chose to walk in, instead of walking in His ways. I did it internally, knowing that it was not pleasing to God and, for that reason, I cannot and will never get anymore tattoos or piercings.

"The Lord says, 'The women of Zion are haughty, walking along with outstretched necks, flirting with their eyes, strutting along with swaying hips, with ornaments jingling on their ankles. Therefore the Lord will bring sores on the heads of the women of Zion; the Lord will make their scalps bald.'
In that day the Lord will snatch away their finery: the bangles and headbands and crescent necklaces, the earrings and bracelets and veils, the headdresses and anklets and sashes, the perfume bottles and charms, the signet rings and nose

rings, the fine robes and the capes and cloaks, the
purses and mirrors, and the linen garments and
tiaras and shawls.
Instead of fragrance there will be a stench;
instead of a sash, a rope;
instead of well-dressed hair, baldness;
instead of fine clothing, sackcloth;
instead of beauty, branding."
Isaiah 3:16-24 (NIV)

These verses depict the very way I acted in
the eyes of the Lord, and just as He says in this
scripture, I thought I looked good. I was haughty,
stuck up, and I thought I had it going on, but it
was stench in the nostrils of God.

My newfound love for sin and the pleasures
of the nightlife caused me to act as if I were child-
less. I disregarded my children, leaving them
with their father almost every weekend. I tried to
justify it by saying to myself that I was teaching
him a lesson. I wanted to make him feel what it
was like to take care of the kids on his own, but I
didn't think about the pain it was inflicting on my
innocent children.

When my mom found out about our separation, she drove out to where I lived; this was about an hour from her home. She pleaded with me to stop all the craziness, but I let everything she said go in one ear and out the other. I told her that I was going to file for divorce. She was so devastated, but not as devastated as my next decision would make her.

CHAPTER 10

Generational Curses

Lust is never satisfied. No matter how much you attempt to gratify the pleasures of the flesh, lust devours and demands more. I heard a woman of God use an acrostic for lust and it is:

Living

Under

Satan's

Torment

This was the case after I moved out of the home I shared with my husband. I lived a lascivious lifestyle. I was drinking heavily, dabbling in drugs and fornicating. I thought I was having the time of my life, but little did I know the cost and torment that would be my harvest. The Message Bible describes lust this way:

> *"Hell has a voracious appetite,*
> *and lust just never quits."*
> *Proverbs 27:20 (MSG)*

Pretty soon, my weekend partying became my way of life. I began dating a guy and I lied to him about being married and about having four children. I would be over his house all the time— sometimes overnight. This meant that my kids were with my estranged husband a lot. My children felt the pain from my actions in their own ways, but my youngest (my then four-year-old daughter, Elizabeth) was very confused and sad almost all the time. She would cry every time I dropped her off with her dad. She would cling to me and ask me when I would pick her up. I was very vague with my answers to her because I honestly didn't know. I did whatever I felt like for the moment and dealt with the consequences later. Her cries did not stop me from leaving her. Sure, I felt guilty at the moment, but my own desires to fulfill the emptiness inside me were more important. I thought that the emptiness could only be filled by men, the attention I received from them, the alcohol I'd come to love and the partying lifestyle I'd come to depend on. This is why I can understand how some women can put these things before their kids, even though others cannot. I'm not condoning this type of behavior by a woman, but what I am saying is that I understand it. In my own experience, it was like there was a driving force on the inside of me and I felt compelled to appease it. I felt as if I needed these things in my life to be fulfilled and accepted.

My estranged husband was struggling financially. We were constantly struggling, but with him suddenly living off one income, it was evident that it was too much to maintain. He came and begged me to reconcile. He told me that he still loved me and that we could work things out. He tried his best to convince me, but I wasn't hearing it. I wanted nothing to do with him. Honestly, as much as it hurts to say this: at that time in my life, I wished that I was single and free. Single—as in divorced already and free—as in free from the responsibilities of being a mother. This is where the generational curse of abandonment came into play in my life. Generational curses are curses that affect us, but they enter into our lives through inheritance. They are the result of sins committed by the generations before us. John Eckhardt defines a curse this way: *God's recom-*

*pense in the life of a person and his or her descen-
dants as a result of iniquity. The curse causes sorrow of the heart and gives demonic spirits legal
entry into a family whereby they can carry out
and perpetuate their wicked devices (Identifying
and Breaking Curses).* My father abandoned me
and suddenly, I was doing the same to my children. Generational curses are an ongoing cycle
that affects many generations to come. The very
action of sin that caused the curse to fall upon
the previous generation and the present generation will repeat itself, thus cursing the generations to come. It is yet another way that the enemy gets into the bloodline, whereby, securing his
evil works through the person and their seed.

Abandonment by a parent opens a child up
and gives an illegal spirit legal entry by which to
enter. That is how I was opened up to the spirit of
rejection and now, the next generation (my children) were going through the same thing. Anytime we make a choice to sin, we move out from
under the blessings of God and invite a curse to
be established in our families. The demonic kingdom doesn't overlook any opportunity to kill,

steal, and destroy.

"Anyone who does not provide for their relatives, and especially for their own household, has denied the faith and is worse than an unbeliever."
1 Timothy 5:8 (NIV)

I didn't see the hurt that my actions were causing my children. I was too wrapped up in my own selfishness. My boys began acting out in school. They were fighting and even got suspended a few times. My youngest son was a "stuffer." He stuffed all his feelings, so he would isolate himself from others. My daughter would just cry, and all my husband and I could seem to do was argue and fight. History seemed to be repeating itself. Just as my mother and father were in their own vortex of pain and wrapped up in their hurts, my husband and I were repeating the same offense. We were fighting and arguing while the enemy was busy at work sowing tares into our children.

If you take a moment and look back on the history of your family, I'm sure that many of you will see a pattern of generational curses in your own family. There are many types of generation curses. Things such as poverty, divorce, depression, anger, and depression seem to run in families and are often generational curses. The world says that all these are learned patterns of behavior. The Bible teaches us that the sins of the father can visit the third and fourth generations.

"The Lord your God, am a jealous God, punishing the children for the sin of the parents to the third and fourth generation of those who hate me."
Exodus 20:5 (NIV)

Derek Prince listed seven common indications (not proofs) of a curse operating in the bloodline in his book, *Blessing or Curse* and they are:
1. Chronic Financial Problems
2. Chronic Sickness and Disease
3. Female Problems (also barrenness)
4. Accident Proneness
5. Marital Problems
6. Premature death and
7. Mental Illness

Sin that opens the door in one generation can become a generational curse to the next *(Derek Prince, Blessing or Curse).*

So, my father's choice to sin and my choice to sin and move out of God's blessings and protection, invited a curse to further be established in my family.

When my husband realized that I wasn't going to be moving back home, he decided to move back to Georgia with his parents. This is where an idea entered into my mind; I saw an opportunity to get free from my responsibilities as a mother. I told him that the kids needed him and it wasn't fair to just leave me in California all alone to raise them. I put such a guilt trip on him that I convinced him to take the kids with him to Georgia under the pretense that I would move back there after I saved up some money from my new job. I told him that I would come and join them in a few months. I led my husband on about the possibility of us reconciling. I did this to get what I wanted, but at the time, I had no intentions of reconciling.

Shortly after he agreed to pack up the kids and take them with him, we had a garage sale at the old house. My children wept as they watched strangers pick through the items that once filled the place they called home. It was devastating to them. We were all very sad. For a brief moment, I started feeling like I was making a huge mistake, but those feelings were quickly dismissed when I received a call from the boyfriend I was entertaining at the moment. "I couldn't change the plan now," I said to myself. "I'll never be free if he doesn't take the kids." It sounds terrible, but that was my main focus: me. All I could think of was my needs, my wants, and my freedom.

I packed the last few belongings my children had back at my apartment and drove them to a fast food restaurant where we were to meet their father. The children cried again and said their goodbyes to me. I made them promises that I halfheartedly meant. My baby girl still didn't quite understand what exactly was taking place, but the shock of her reality would soon be discovered. All of them would soon realize that I had abandoned them. How, as a mother, could I do this to my children? How could I abandon them, being a child who'd experienced firsthand the same thing done by my father? My answer is simple: hurt people, hurt people. My other explanation is that my appetite for sin was furious and my selfish desires just wouldn't quit.

CHAPTER 11

Broad is the Road that Leads to Destruction

My lifestyle became even crazier after I didn't have my kids with me. The relationship that I so desperately wanted to work that I'd abandoned my children for fell completely apart. I became very depressed, so I partied even harder and drank even heavier. I eventually lost my job and couldn't afford to pay my rent. I scammed my way into a new apartment, but when the rent started piling up there, I became desperate.

The guilt of abandoning my children was eating me alive. I would drive out to our old house and park in front of the house. I would sit there, reminisce and weep for hours. I knew I had made a huge mistake. I knew the enemy had robbed me and I'd allowed him to do it. I felt so defeated and so alone. I was miserable without my kids. I decided that I was going to do whatever I had to do to fly out there and get them back. I wanted my family back. I wanted my life back, but it was all gone. The spirit of discouragement, shame, regret and grief joined the party in my soul. I was a mess.

One night, I went out clubbing with some friends and I met a man. We went back to my house and I confided in him about my financial struggles. The next morning, he started telling me that he had the answers to all my financial problems. He told me that I should start escorting. He told me that all I had to do was meet with some lonely, older men— men who simply wanted company, and I would be paid up to a couple hundred dollars an hour. I was naïve so I believed him and I agreed to do it. He told me that we should go to a different city so no one would recognize me or know who I was. It all sounded so innocent and harmless, plus, I was going to be losing my apartment soon, so I needed to get the rent paid. I also reasoned in my mind that if I was going to get to my children, it was going to cost money and I needed to get to them by any means necessary.

It was very apparent to me on the very first "date" that there was more expected of me than dinner and a movie. I realized that the man I had trusted to help me with my financial problems was nothing more than a pimp. I was far away from home and he had driven us to the city that I was escorting in, so I was stuck. After about a week and after the money started coming in, he became possessive and increasingly violent. I started devising a plan of escape from him. I stayed with him for about a month, working and stashing money. By this time, he was limiting my phone calls and screening who I called, so I wasn't even calling my kids daily like I usually did. I caught onto what he was doing and how he was getting the "clients," so I realized that I didn't need him taking any part of my money anymore. When I had saved up a good sum of money, I ran away. Instead of running home and back to safety, I decided that I would continue escorting. I hired a couple of guys to be my body guards and recruited a couple of other women who desperately needed money and were willing to escort to get it. For three months straight, we worked around the clock. This was my crew; there were no pimps, no one taking anyone's money and no one being abused. The girls kept their money and we paid the men a set price for being our body guards. In return, they ensured our safety. The money was crazy. I had more money than I'd ever had, but the emptiness and shame I felt from selling my body was unbearable and alcohol wasn't numbing it anymore. I started to dabble in prescription drugs. I couldn't even look at myself in the mirror anymore. I was so ashamed of what I had become. Sex, to me, was no longer something to be shared between two people who loved each other; it was power and wealth. Honestly, the hurt that I felt from the rape that took my virginity distorted my view of sex. Sex, to me, was an ugly act. The only reason I was intimate with a man was because I felt accepted and loved by him while in the act, but for the men, it all was about the pleasure. They had no genuine feelings for me. I remember feeling very ashamed, but at the same time, empowered by being an escort. I felt that I had control over the men. They were paying me. I was in charge. I had the power.

These were all lies from the pit of hell. I had no control. The enemy was in full control of my life. I was operating under the spirits of lust, perversion, seduction and others. I was living under Satan's torment and the more I gave myself to those demons, the more I became callous to the things of God.

After a few months, everyone had stacked up a good little amount of money, but I got greedy. I knew that it was only a matter of time before we got caught. If the cops didn't bust us, I knew that one of the local pimps would take me out. I was what you called a renegade because I had no pimp. The other pimps didn't take too kindly to renegades.

One night, I told one of the bodyguards that we should pack up and go home. I got a call for an "out call date." I didn't usually go to a person's place of residence; they usually came to me, but the money being offered was way too much for me to turn down. As my bodyguard and I pulled up to the home, he told me that he'd left his pistol back at the hotel room by accident. I gave him a dirty look, got out of the car and walked up to the doorway of an apartment located behind some storefront building. I knocked on the door and it halfway opened. I called out into a semi-dark room that was lit by a neon blue light from a huge fish aquarium. That aquarium stood half the height of the living room wall. I could see a tall shadowy figure seated on the couch and he motioned for me to come in. I came in and shut the door behind me. As I walked in closer, he motioned to the hundred dollars bills lying on the glass coffee table. I quickly walked over to grab them, but just as I extended my arm to get the money, he slammed his pistol down on top of it. He told me to sit down on the couch and then, he began to tell me a story. He started explaining to me that they didn't like what I was doing in their city and that I needed to be taught a lesson. Then he picked up the gun and pointed it at my right temple. My mind raced as I tried to figure out what I should do. All I could remember was my body guard telling me that he had forgotten his weapon back at the hotel. If I screamed and he ran in, he would be unarmed and surely get shot. I could no longer hear what the man was saying.

All I could think about was my children and how
if I were to die, they would be orphans. Although
I was more afraid than I had ever been in my life,
I pretended that I wasn't. The last sentence I
heard the man speak is "...and when I'm done
raping you, I'm going to kill you." These words
rang in my mind as he put the gun down and told
me to get up and take off my clothes. I was so
scared that I couldn't move. I didn't budge, so his
voice got louder and then, he screamed at me to
get up. Still, I didn't move. Instead, in my mind, I
just kept thinking, "Oh, please God, I don't want
to die. Please help me." My life literally flashed
before my eyes and all I could think about was
that I was going to die in a storefront apartment
as a no-name prostitute that some crazy john had
murdered. I said no words but my heart begged
God to help me. I could feel the barrel of the gun
jabbing me in the temple and all I could do was
close my eyes and think about the things that
made me happy. My children and my family
played over and over in my head. Just then, the
man heard a noise outside. When his attention
was brought back to me, his demeanor had completely changed. He stopped yelling at me, leaned

into my ear and made this threat. He said, "If you work another day in my city or if I find out that you are still here after tonight, I'm going to bust you." *Bust me? How could he bust me?* I was confused until he pulled his wallet out and showed me his badge. He told me that they had been watching me do my own thing, making money without paying "them" any dues. "Who do you think you are?" he proceeded to ask me. "You're working in my city, but not paying me what is due me." Then he raised his voice again and told me to get the hell out of his face and I gladly took off running towards the door. I ran through the door and into the night. This incident took me back in time to when I was 13 years old and running from my rapist. That was the spirit of fear resurfacing and rearing up its ugly head once again in my life. I was 13 years old all over again and reliving one of the most horrific times in my life. I spotted the car with my body guard sitting in the front seat sound asleep. He must have seen the fear on my face as I jumped in the car because he immediately demanded me to tell him what happened. All I could say was "DRIVE!" He slammed on the gas and we peeled out of there. I was in shock. There was no way that I had just escaped death. My heart was pounding as I told my body guard all that had taken place. He was furious. When we got back to the hotel, he grabbed his pistol and told me to stay there with the other girls and he would handle everything. After he had left, I went into the bathroom where no one could hear me, closed the door behind me, sat on the cold tile floor, buried my face into my hands and wept. I decided right then that I was done with that lifestyle. Deep down inside, I knew that if I were to continue with that lifestyle, I would eventually end up dead. I counted up the money I had on me and promised myself that in the morning, I would head straight to the bank and deposit it with the other money I had saved. I would then head back home to my normal life.

The next day, I was awakened by my body-guard coming in the hotel room. He had just re-turned. He assured me all had been dealt with and that I didn't have to worry about anything. I told him about my decision. I told him I could not do escorting anymore. He argued with me that everything was fine now and that we wouldn't

have any problems from that guy or anyone else.
I insisted that I was done. I told the girls to get
their belongings because we were packing up
and checking out. My bodyguard was upset. He
told me that I was stupid to be walking away
from all the money that was to be made. I explained to him that it was my life at risk, not his,
so he needed to back off because I had already
made my decision. Just then, the pre-paid phone
rang—the one we only used to set up dates. My
bodyguard answered it and shoved it in my face.
He mouthed the words, "One last call." I hesitated, but then answered with a "Hello." The caller
on the other end explained that he wanted a date
with me. I agreed to meet with him and in thirty
minutes, I was awaiting his arrival at my hotel
room. My bodyguard sent me a text message,
telling me that my date was coming up the stairs.
I heard a knock on the hotel door and as I walked
to the door to open it, my phone began to ring. I
ignored it, not knowing it was my bodyguard trying to warn me to not open the door. I was too
late. As soon as I opened the door, the police
rushed in and bombarded the room. The next
hour consisted of me being searched, questioned

and then, I was arrested. *Talk about a walk of shame.* Every guest at the hotel was outside of their hotel rooms pointing at me as I was hand-cuffed, escorted down the stairs and placed in the back of the police car. I was booked for solicitation of prostitution and spent the night in jail. The spirit of shame screamed in my head as I sat in that jail cell. "You are nothing but a whore. You are exactly what every parent hopes their daughter never becomes. You are disgusting. You are nothing but trash." The spirit of shame and condemnation was so heavy on me that I felt like the scum of the earth. The correctional officer read my charges out loud in front of everyone in the jail cell as they called my name to fingerprint and strip search me. Their eyes of judgment pierced through me, but the spirit of pride in me reacted with attitude and cockiness.

"And ye are puffed up, and have not rather mourned, that he that hath done this deed might be taken away from among you."
1 Corinthians 5:2 (KJV)

The spirit of pride is a cover up for rejection.

Pride is a form of self-love. Arrogance and cockiness is a person's way of self-loving themselves to cover up their feelings of rejection. Someone who constantly operates in the spirit of pride and is arrogant needs deliverance from the strong-man of rejection as well. The Bible warns us about the outcome of pride if we choose to walk in it.

> *"Pride goeth before destruction and a haughty spirit before a fall."*
> *Proverbs 16:18 (KJV)*

I had enough money to bail myself out, so I was released the next day. The money I'd planned to put in the bank was confiscated at the hotel room. I still had some money in the bank, but because of my arrest, I could not leave the state of California. This put me in a great depression. I longed to go get my kids back and restore the family that I'd lost. My boys would write me letters, asking why I had left them and when I was coming for them. My four-year-old daughter wasn't speaking. She had completely shut down and would no longer talk at home or at school.

Everyone was concerned about her. No one could comprehend why I didn't just fly to Georgia and get my kids. Of course, I was too ashamed and prideful to tell anyone about the trouble I had gotten into with the law. After nine months of court hearings and sentencing, I took a plea bargain, did my time and within twenty-four hours of being told I was free to leave the state, I was flying out to Georgia to get my children. I was determined to move out there and put that situation behind me. I wanted to treat it as if it never happened. Unfortunately, changing destinations does not faze the enemy or any demons one bit. I could have moved a million times and it would not have mattered. I needed deliverance, not a new address.

When I arrived in Georgia, my husband and I agreed that we would try to work things out. I didn't tell him anything about me being an escort or the trouble I had gotten myself into. I saw no need for it and frankly, I thought that all it would have done was hinder any chance of reconciliation, plus, I was too ashamed. I used the money I had saved up and found us a house. My husband was already working a good job with the airlines and I began working as a retail manager. The kids were in school, my daughter was speaking again and everything seemed to be getting back to normal. The only thing was I'd resisted allowing God back into my life. I had no desire to go to church.

During the week, my husband and I worked and on the weekends, we partied. We partied together, we partied separate and we both drank a lot. The boys had become teenagers and were old enough to look after my daughter, so they were home alone most of the time. Our marriage bed was ice cold. I had a lot of shame because of what I had done. Sex was even more distorted and this made it almost impossible for me to be intimate with him. We were just going through the motions of life. I was no longer the same person. I had experienced too much and the things in the world had changed me. I felt corrupted and defiled. I was no longer the woman my husband had married. Our marriage began to suffer again and when I found out my husband was seeing a woman at work, things fell completely apart. I went on week-long drinking sprees. I started partying with the owners of a cellular company I worked for. They knew a lot of people in the hip hop scene, so we partied all over Atlanta. I sure thought I was something, partying with celebrities, drinking, smoking and completely out of control again. My husband was doing the same thing with his buddies. Again, my children suffered alone and were unsupervised. Either we were home arguing about everything and anything or we were gone, leaving our children to care for themselves. After two years of this, my husband and I decided once again that we would stop all our partying ways (this time for good) and wholeheartedly attempt to make our marriage work. So in 2008, we packed up all our belongings, quit our jobs, gathered up our children and moved back to California.

Once in California, my mom and stepdad welcomed us into their home. The kids were thrilled to be back with the family. It wasn't long before me and my husband's old habits returned and within months of moving in my parent's home, we were out partying while my parents cared for our kids. One night while I was driving home from clubbing with the girls, the police pulled me over and I was arrested for DUI (driving under the influence). My husband bailed me out, but my behavior afterwards didn't get better; instead, it grew worse. I was out almost every night.

One particular night, I followed my husband because I suspected that he was seeing someone else and my worst fears were confirmed. I found him with another woman at a nightclub. I had a total breakdown. I was so hurt and broken that I decided I was done with the marriage. I went to the courthouse and filed for divorce the following week. My hurt was overwhelming, but I didn't know what to do to ease the pain so I drank, did drugs and partied. I began drinking to the point of blacking out. This was the case on one particular night.

Some of my girlfriends and I went out to dinner and then, to a nightclub. I began drinking shots at the bar and when I woke up, I was in the passenger's side of my car and my friend, who was supposed to be my designated driver, was being arrested for a DUI. I was confused and didn't understand what was going on. The police officer was trying his best to explain the situation. He told me that he couldn't release my car to me and let me drive home because I had been drinking. He told me that my car needed to remain parked there in the restaurant parking lot until the morning when I had sobered up. Then I could get it. When I asked the officer how I was going to get home, he motioned to a car parked a few spaces down and told me that my friends had agreed to give me a ride home. I looked over to where the officer had motioned and saw the female bartender that had been serving us drinks at the bar earlier. While being arrested, my friend said that she knew her and that she would make sure that I got home safe. I was confused and still trying to piece together what was going on. I staggered over to the driver's side of the woman's car and the woman rolled down her window. "Hey girl!" she said. "Jump on in. I'll give you a ride home." I looked in the back seat of the car and saw two men I didn't know and another man in the passenger's seat. She must have seen the look of hesitation on my face because she went on to say, "Oh girl, don't mind them. These are just my homeboys. We're about to smoke and then, take you home after all these cops leave. So just get your stuff, and in the morning, I can bring you back to your car." Everything in me told me to run away, but what other choice did I have? I thought about calling my parents, but I couldn't locate my purse or my phone. My friend told me that I'd lost my phone and my purse at the club. I had either dropped it or someone must have stolen it from me when I was passed out.

The police put my friend in the back of the police car, told me to lock up my car and told me that they would keep my keys in custody. This was to ensure that I didn't attempt to drive my car while drunk. They said that I could pick my keys up in the morning at the police station. I hesitantly walked over to the woman's car and got in the backseat. I was immediately handed a bottle of Hennessy; I took two long shots and passed out again. When I woke up, my head was spinning and I was nowhere near home. From what I could make out, we were in some sort of underground parking garage. It reeked of marijuana, so I knew that they had just finished smoking. When I began questioning them about where we were, the men told me to shut up. The woman who had been driving was getting off the car. "Well, I gotta get up early y'all. Goodnight," she said. That's when I realized that we were in her apartment's garage. I quickly rolled down the window and caught her arm as she walked by. "You promised me that you would get me home safe, girl. Please don't leave me here with these guys." When I saw the coldness in her eyes, I began to panic. "Please," I begged her. "Please let me stay with you and spend the night at your spot. I'll take a taxi in the morning and get my car." She coldly took my hand off her arm and said, "Girl, they are going to take you home. They just stopped to drop me off." I knew she was lying. Just then, one of the men told me to get out that car and motioned for me to get into a different one. I refused and one of the men began shouting at me. I began to cry because I knew they were going to hurt me. The man threatened me. He said that as soon as he was done smoking, I had better be in the other car. I was afraid, so I quickly began to devise a getaway plan. I kicked my heels off. I planned to run while the men were occupied with their smoking. I waited until the right moment and pulled the door handle to open the door, but to my disappointment, it didn't budge. The child safety lock was on. I reached over the opened window and pulled the door handle from the outside and the door popped open. That's when I took off running. I found myself running once more, running from harm, running from the next assault. I was thirteen again, running from my rapist and scared out of my mind. One of the men began chasing me. He was gaining on me and before long, he'd caught up with me. He grabbed me by my hair and dragged me across the parking garage and back to the car. He didn't put me back in the car though. He told the other men to get in the car and shut the doors. He took me around the back of the car and shoved my face down onto the closed trunk of the car and began to pull down my pants from behind. When I wouldn't open my legs to make it easier for him, he kicked the inside of my left leg with his timberland boot and I felt a surge of pain go up my leg and into my back. It felt like he had broken it. I fought him off as much as I could, but eventually, I grew tired and gave in. He raped me on the back of that car in the garage that night. I blacked out again, but this time, it wasn't because of alcohol; it was because of fear.

When I awoke, I was being yelled at and the man who raped me was demanding that I tell him where I lived so he could drop me off. In my mind, I knew there was no way in the world I was going to tell him where I lived, so I gave him directions that landed me about two blocks from my home. When we pulled up to the curb, the man yelled, "Get out!" I walked two blocks to my street, walked into my home, and collapsed in my bed. My mind was spinning and I was exhausted but relieved to be home and safe at last.

I woke up about four hours later to a friend of mine who had been with us the night before pounding on my door. She was worried because she hadn't heard from me or the other friend who had been arrested. When I told her what all had occurred, she asked me if I had showered yet and I told her that I hadn't. I had been too exhausted and told her I was pretty sure I was drugged earlier by the female bartender, since she was the one pouring our shots. I told her about how I had drank Hennessy out of a bottle they had in their car and how sure I was that it had been drugged as well. She began to sob. When I heard the story relayed in my own voice, it because so real to me that I began to sob uncontrollably as well. She got me up out of bed and rushed me to the hospital. The police were called and I contacted my lawyer that was working on my current DUI case. I told him all the details and about how I'd been raped the night before. I asked him for advice. My fear was this: the fact that I had been in a club and drunk in public, which were both two separate violations of my bond, that it would negatively affect my upcoming court hearing. He gave me the news that I was dreading to hear. He told me that although he would never advise me not to report a rape, he did want me to completely understand the consequences that may come from going forward with the charges and when all the details surrounding the rape came to light in court. I explained to him that I was the victim and he said to me that although I was the victim, that many times in rape cases where there are no other witnesses and alcohol is involved, it boils down to "he said, she said." The most credible one is usually the one the jury or judge believes. He said that my credibility was not the best and that he would strongly suggest that I weigh out my decision carefully, realizing there would be backlash, possibly even a guilty charge or at least a violation in my current case. I hung up the phone, buried my face in my hands, and cried. I was so hurt and angry. I felt the spirit of anger rise up from inside me, along with bitterness and hate. I felt like I was the thirteen year old girl again, back with that youth pastor and listening to him explain to me all the reasons why I shouldn't tell. I was hearing, once again, how I should just keep my mouth shut and take it. I needed to just hang my head down and accept the rape. My thoughts waged war in my head. The demonic spirits pierced my very soul with their vile words. "So what? You were raped again." The horrific thoughts got worse and echoed in my mind, "So what, you were violated and so what, you've been disgraced. No one cares. You're nothing.

God doesn't even care about you and that's why He keeps letting you get hurt. He doesn't love you and why would He love you? You are disgusting. So just shut up and take it. You deserve it anyway because you're nothing more than a whore, ex-prostitute, alcoholic and a drug addicted piece of trash. This is what you deserve. No one will ever believe a whore like you could have been raped anyway." I cried and held myself knowing that I was completely helpless again. I knew once my previous record came to light showing the prostitution charges and the toxicology report proving that I had been drinking, taking Xanax, using Meth and smoking marijuana, no jury would believe me. A new level of anger took root in me that day. The spirits of wrath, hate, self-hate and murder entered in. I wanted to kill my rapist and I wanted to kill myself. I hated myself and I was fiercely angry at the world and there was nothing I could do about it. I was going to have to keep silent again. I walked out of the hospital room and told my friend who was waiting in the ER lobby that I was done. I asked her to please take me to her house because I didn't want to face my family or answer any questions about what had happened to me. I cried and cried as I got in the shower that evening. As every bit of evidence of the rape went down the drain, I felt as though my very life was going down with it.

CHAPTER 12

From Bad to Worst

Just as I had once acted out, isolated myself and rebelled after my first rape, I did so after the second one. After the rape, I never returned home. My family was very worried about me and once again, my children were tossed to the side. I just couldn't bring myself to return home and face them all. I knew that if they began questioning me about that night, I would completely lose my mind. I stayed with the friend who had taken me to the hospital for a few weeks and then, I couch-hopped, living at different friends' homes until I eventually ended up living in my car. I got another DUI, but this time, I had blacked out behind the wheel at a red light with my foot on the brake. When the cops pulled up, witnesses at a nearby home said I had been there for over an hour. I went to jail again, but bailed out unfazed and headed right to the nearest bar.

One night while at a bar, I met a man (we will call him Timothy). We got drunk, we got high and I confided in him about the rape. He told me that he was going to take care of me and that everything was going to be okay. He told me that I didn't have to live out of my car anymore. Within two weeks, we were living together. Things seemed to be going well for a short period of time. I came around to visit my family and since I had a stable place to live, I started getting my daughter on the weekends. My sons wanted nothing to do with me and I completely understand their reasons for feeling that way. I had hurt them very much. I had rejected them. I had chosen men and my crazy lifestyle over them, and just when they would try and allow me back into their lives, I would do it all over again to them. Their hearts just couldn't take it anymore. It reminds me of a study done on children that experienced maternal separation and deprivation in their infancy. The study concluded that that these children went through three different and distinct stages once separated from their mothers. Those stages were:

- **(First) Protest**: The child cries, screams

and protests angrily when the parent leaves. They will try to cling and hold on to the parent to stop them from leaving.

- **(Second) Despair**: The child's protesting begins to stop and they appear to be calmer, although still upset. The child refuses others' attempts for comfort and often seems withdrawn and uninterested in anything.

- **(Third) Detachment**: If separation continues, the child will start to engage with other people again. They will reject the parent on their return and show strong signs of anger.

Study conducted by Robertson and Bowlby (1952).

My boys had detached from me and even though it grieved me, I continued in the very behavior that broke their hearts. This allowed the cycle to continue, thus allowing the enemy's demonic plan for our lives to remain on course. Our lives reflected that quite clearly by the state of utter chaos we lived in.

It wasn't long before my new boyfriend and I began to fight and argue. If you put two alcoholic drug addicts in a relationship, there will be much destruction. He began to punch and hit me during his drunken rages. I would hide from family for weeks due to black eyes and bruises on my face and body. It was like my first marriage all over again, but this time, drugs and alcohol were involved. My parents begged me to leave him. My children begged me to leave as well, but I was stuck once again in "battered woman syndrome." Not only did I feel I wouldn't leave him, but I felt as though I couldn't leave him. After being thrown out of multiple apartments due to domestic violence complaints, my parents, who were still caring for all my children, told me that for my daughter's safety, she could no longer visit me until I could provide a safe place for her— free of violence. They even came to my apartment with a moving truck and helped me move all my belongings out of his apartment, only for me to return to him two days later. The shame and the stupidity of my actions drove me to drink even more. I began to drink at home alone. Timothy kept me isolated and wouldn't let me have any friends outside our relationship. He cut me off from everyone. I was alone, drinking and using cocaine, Meth pills or anything I could get my hands on. I used these substances more than I had ever done before in my life. After finding out that Timothy was cheating on me with a girl I'd caught him with one night, we had a huge fight. During that fight, he punched me in my face with such force that I was knocked unconscious. I awoke two hours later. I couldn't see out of my left eye, but I was able to find my spare car key. I managed to walk downstairs to the garage where my Mercedes was parked, but it wasn't there. Timothy had taken it. Picturing him and this new girlfriend out in my car enraged me. I called my soon-to-be ex-husband and told him to please come get me and he did. I arrived at my mother's house and my mom began to weep when she saw my face all black and blue and my left eye swollen shut. It was like I was back in time again, reliving my first marriage. I was reminded of the day that my mom came to get me 20 years prior to this incident. I was in the same, if not worse, situation. I asked myself: *Why, oh why do I keep going in these same circles? Why do I keep finding myself in these situations?* I sounded like the Israelites when they murmured and complained to God about all they were enduring in the wilderness. Of course, it was their bad decisions and disobedience that kept them wandering.

"And the LORD spoke to me, saying, you have cir-cled this mountain long enough. Now turn north."
Deuteronomy 2:2 (NAS)

"He has known your wanderings through this great wilderness. These forty years the LORD your God has been with you; you have not lacked a thing."
Deuteronomy 2:7 (NAS)

The reason I continued to wander and experience the torment of the enemy was because I was away from God. He hadn't moved. I had moved and the consequence of that move was that I was out of His protection because of my own sinful desires. Satan and his demons had all power to torment me. I was wide open, uncovered and un-protected, so what I was experiencing was a di-rect harvest of my wrong decisions. Howbeit, my choices weren't just affecting me; everyone around me was touched by my actions.

I decided to report my car stolen, so I called 911 and the police came out to make a report. However, when the police officers got to my parents' house, they were more concerned about what happened to my face than a report of a stolen car. After they questioned me for a while, I finally admitted that my boyfriend had beaten me up. For safety reasons, they took me down to the station. After I finished the report, they took me to the hospital. The police officers went to our apartment to arrest my boyfriend, but Timothy resisted arrest and ended up barricading himself inside the apartment. Because there were weapons in the apartment, the police had to proceed with caution. After a four-and-a-half hour standoff with the SWAT team, they were finally able to arrest him and take him into custody. While in the hospital, I started receiving treatment for my eye. Due to the impact, my eye's retina had detached itself. I was placed on a lot of heavy medication, including pain meds. With my now ex-boyfriend in jail and awaiting a court hearing for the battery charge, my parents allowed me to have custody of my daughter again. I was so traumatized by all that happened that in order to cope, I began to drink even more. I would drink from the moment I woke up until I took my daughter to school. I would drink all day while she was at school and I would pick her up drunk and bring her back home. I was physically there, but I was not emotionally present in her life. I started to blackout earlier and earlier in the evenings, which meant that my daughter was left to care for herself. There were many times when I would wake up in the early morning hours, re-membering nothing about the night before. When I was asleep, she could not wake me up, no matter how hard she tried. She would do her best to care for herself, pick out her clothes for school the next day, do her homework, make her-self dinner and put herself to bed. Things got progressively worse over the next few months. My daughter even started acting out in school. My reaction to her reaction was I would drink more.

On Labor Day, I received bad news that a close friend of mine, who was like a mother to me, had passed away. She had been in and out of the hospital due to illness and I'd seen her about a week prior to her death. On that last visit, she had a heart-to-heart with me about my drinking. I attempted to quit after our talk. I managed to remain sober for just over a week and I had fallen off the wagon a day prior to her passing. When I heard the news, I started drinking even more, and at some point while in an active blackout, I made the decision to drive to go be with the family. They lived in a city about an hour away from where I lived. I put my daughter in the backseat of my car and started driving. I hadn't even driven a mile away from my house when a police officer spotted me swerving and attempted to pull me over. When I wouldn't pull over, the police report stated that I began to drive recklessly and my daughter jumped out of the car while it was still in motion. At this point, I proceeded to lead police on a low-speed chase. I hit two parked cars which caused me to bounce into oncoming traffic and then, I bounced back into the traffic on the correct side of the street. I continue to drive the car on the rims, tearing up the blacktop. Eventually, the police were able to pull me over. Once they had me stopped, they tried to convince me to get out of the car. When I refused and wouldn't turn the car engine off or exit the vehicle, they pulled me out through the driver's side window. I resisted arrest, fought with the officers, and even spit in one officer's face. They finally had to wrestle me down to the ground to get me in handcuffs. Because I have very small wrists, I managed to get out of the cuffs so they ended up having to hog-tie me, put a spit mask over my face and throw me in the back of the police car. All of this took place right in front of my daughter, who had now been brought to the scene of the accident by the police. Additionally, the wreck took place right in front of the office of Child Protective Services. My daughter was removed from my care. The ambulance treated and released her and I was taken to the hospital. I woke up a few hours later totally unaware of the accident or the fact that I had attempted to drive. When the officers told me what I had done, I thought they were joking; that was, until I saw my arm handcuffed to the hospital bed. The cold reality set in really quick and sobered me up instantly. I realized that I hadn't been that sober in months. Questions went hurling through my mind. I asked the officer if my daughter had been in the car. When he told me that she was, I went ballistic. I demanded he tell me her condition, but he gave me no response and I don't blame him. He was the officer whose face I'd spat in. After I was treated and released, I was taken straight to jail. A day later, I was out on bond awaiting my court date. I was facing some heavy charges. I had a total of ten charges and I was afraid that I was going to go to jail or prison for a very long time. So I did what I always did when I was afraid—I went home and drank. This time though, I didn't have my daughter. This broke my heart. As I sat alone in my apartment, I wept for my daughter and for what my life had become. I finished the rest of the bottle of vodka and called up a local recovery home for women. The woman on the other line asked me if I had been sober for over three days. I lied and said that I had been, so she proceeded to tell me to come in the next morning for intake. I knew I would need my car to get around, so I called a cab in an attempt to go and get my car out of impound. When I got to the impound yard, they told me the car was not able to be driven. I called my insurance and asked them about repairing the car, but they told me the damaged would not be covered under my policy. The reason for this was because I had not disclosed to them that my license had been suspended because of two prior DUI's I had gotten after I'd started the policy with them. I was very upset. I thought about trying to fix it on my own, but decided that I shouldn't risk driving anymore because if I were to get pulled over, I would definitely go straight to jail with no chance of getting my daughter back. So I put my energy into my outpatient treatment because I knew that in order for me to get my daughter back, I was going to have to at least try sobriety. After six months of successful attendance, I was able to have supervised visits with my daughter. After nine months at the program, I was given full custody of my daughter. I was so happy. After a year at the program, I graduated and moved into a sober living home. My daughter and I had our own two bedroom apartment, but we were subject to random search and drug testing. I did well there for a while until I started drinking again. I wasn't worried about getting kicked out because they were randomly drug testing and I was just drinking. I justified my behavior in my mind at first and swore to myself that I would only drink on weekends, but it wasn't long before it became the norm throughout the week. I guess someone must have smelled it on me because one day, the counselor came over and told me she was going to random test me. I asked her for a specimen cup, but instead, she pulled out a breathalyzer. I was shocked. After I failed both attempts, she gave me an ultimatum. Go to detox for 72 hours and sober up or leave within 24 hours. So I ended up going to the 72 hour detox and tried to remain sober. I knew I had to stop drinking, but I just couldn't. That spirit of addiction had made me a slave to alcohol and I kept relapsing. I had an upcoming court date to face on ten charges for the accident involving my daughter. I tried my best to stay sober, but the day before court, I went out drinking and when I arrived at court the next day, I reeked of alcohol. I found out that the judge wanted me to do at least two years in prison or four years in county jail for the accident. The public defender told me that I should just take a plea bargain. I had just landed a great job as an accountant and even though I wasn't sober, my daughter was so happy that we were back together again. I really didn't want to leave her. A close friend of our family who was a private attorney agreed to defend me in my case. Fortunately, she was kind enough to work with me on her fees. That was the Lord's mercy. He was still extending grace to me in the midst of my rebellion.

"But because of his great love for us, God, who is rich in mercy, made us alive with Christ even when we were dead in transgressions—it is by grace you have been saved."
Ephesians 2:4-5 (NIV)

His love and mercy for me were relentless.

The next five weeks before my court date were very scary for me. Not knowing what the future held for me was terrifying. I knew I needed to remain sober, but I would do okay for a few days and then, I'd be drunk again. My parents prayed for me constantly and supported me, along with my aunt and uncle who were pastors at a local church in our city. My lawyer was Christian and was constantly praying for me too. I felt

guilty that I was lying to them all about my sobriety, but I was too afraid of losing my freedom and
my daughter. At this point, I felt like I'd already
lost my sons. They wanted nothing to do with me
and I honestly didn't blame them. The day before
court, I met with my lawyer. She prayed with me
and began going over my case with me. She had
put together a really good case. I felt so thankful
that she'd put so much time and effort into de-
fending me. There were character letters from
friends and family. My Aunt Norma and Uncle
Daniel had written letters as well as my parent's
pastors. I was overwhelmed at their support.

That night, I went out drinking. It was almost
like I wanted to sabotage myself. I felt very guilty
the next morning. I was running around hungover and arrived late to court. I kept telling myself that God would surely bring the hammer
down on me this time. I knew that I was really
sick. I couldn't even stay sober, not even for just
one night. When my name was called, my lawyer,
aunt, uncle and I all stood up. I walked to the
front with my lawyer to hear the judge's decision. I was in shock as he told my lawyer and the

prosecutor that he had never imposed a sentence on anyone who had two prior DUI'S and a child in the car at the time of the third DUI. Nevertheless, he said that he was sentencing me to four months of house arrest and probation. I was so happy, but I didn't understand why the Lord allowed me to go free. I knew I deserved to go to jail or even prison, but in His mercy, He spared me once again. He also spared my daughter from losing her mom again.

I was placed on house arrest for four months and I had to wear an ankle monitor that also detected alcohol. So, I was sober for the next four months and that was the longest I had been sober in a long time. My life seemed to fall back into place during those four months. I began working as an accountant and my daughter and I moved out of sober living and into a regular apartment. It was only a matter of a week after the ankle monitor was off that I decided to be social and join the girls after work for happy hour. It wasn't long before I was skipping the happy hour, buying a bottle of wine after work and drinking it at home. After I had started gaining a lot of weight from drinking wine, I went back to vodka. I would drink before work and immediately after work. Eventually, I started spiking my coffee and sipping it at work. Within three months from the first happy hour, I was in full-blown relapse again. I lost my job and hooked up with a new guy. We created drama in our neighborhood with all the drunken fights I got into with him and my neighbors. I ended up getting my sons caught up in the violence and the chaos of my alcoholic life. When my parents found out I was drinking again and that I'd lost my job, they made a good judgment call and determined that my home was no longer a safe place for my daughter. They came and got her and she began staying at their home again. This gave me a lot of time to drink. I was letting random men stay at my home and I was drinking and mixing pain medications with alcohol. It got to the point where I was so depressed that I didn't even want to get out of bed, change my clothes or even brush my teeth. I wouldn't eat anything; all I would do was lie in bed and drink.

One day, after a week-long binge, I called my

parents. I was drunk and out of my mind. I told them I was going to end my life. They immediately came over and found me. I had taken a half of a bottle of sleeping pills along with vodka. They rushed me to the hospital. After my stomach had been pumped, I was sent home with a doctor's referral to see a psychiatrist. I began seeing him and was placed on anti-depressants and anti-anxiety medications, but I still continued to drink. Additionally, I wasn't sleeping at night, so I was taking tranquilizers nightly and mixing them with vodka. I would sleep three and four days at a time. My mom would come and check on me and even try to bring my daughter to see me, but I was slowly drinking myself to death. Every day, my mom would stop by my home on her way home from work and drop off dinner and every day, she would see the dinner she had left for me the day prior still sitting on the table where she'd left it.

One day, I was outside on the lawn of my apartment drunk and fist fighting one of the neighbors. I staggered back into the house and passed out on the bed. I woke up a few hours later to pounding on my door. It was the landlord telling me to start looking for another place to live because they were going to kick me out. I slammed the door in his face, went into the kitchen and pulled the vodka bottle out of the cupboard. I poured a big shot and swallowed it and then proceeded into the bathroom. As I washed my hands, I looked up into the bathroom mirror and made eye contact with myself. My face was all bruised up and my previously in-jured eye was almost swollen shut again. As I gazed at the reflection staring at me in the mir-ror, I felt nothing but disgust. My skin tone had a yellow tint and the white of my eyes was also yel-low. My hair looked a mess and my clothes hadn't been changed in days. I hated what I had become. I had lost everything. I had lost my family, my job, and everything was falling to pieces around me. I began to cry, but pushed those emotions down as anger began to rise up. I started throwing things around my apartment and ripping pictures off the wall. I was hurt and angry and I just wanted the pain to end. I decided that unlike the last time, I was going to be sure that I completed the task of ending my life once and for all. I poured a

12-ounce glass to the rim with straight 101 proof vodka and took as many tranquilizers as I could shovel into my mouth. Right before I swallowed the pills, I said these words in my mind: *Oh God, forgive me for taking my life, but I'm tired and I want it all to stop. Please forgive me.* I guzzled down the pills with the vodka and just as my head began to spin, I started singing this song in my heart:

> *What can wash away my sin?*
> *Nothing but the blood of Jesus;*
> *What can make me whole again?*
> *Nothing but the blood of Jesus.*
> *Oh precious is the flow*
> *That makes me white as snow;*
> *No other fount I know,*
> *Nothing but the blood of Jesus.*

My children's faces flashed in my mind and I started weeping, knowing that I would never see them again. I told myself that their lives would be better off without me in it. I was no good. All I did was hurt them. They deserved to be happy and free from the disappointments I kept bringing them. I began to lose consciousness and the next thing I remember was waking up in another hospital bed. My feeling of utter disappointment was beyond words. I thought to myself, "My God, am I actually still alive? When will this nightmare end?" I was shocked that I was still breathing. A nurse walked into my room to see if I had regained consciousness. I asked her for some water, but she ignored me and walked out of the hospital room. I didn't blame them for being tired of seeing me. I was in and out of the hospital. I yelled for her to bring me my phone, but when she didn't return and I couldn't find the nurse's call button, I started taking the intravenous needles out of my arm and I attempted to get out of the hospital bed. My stomach was hurting and my head was pounding. I could still taste the charcoal in my mouth from them pumping my stomach. I found my clothes and my phone and called my mom. Her and my stepdad came to the hospital and picked me up. My mom pleaded with me to come back to her home and stay with them, but that was the last thing I wanted to do. All I could think about was getting home so I could drink since obviously, I couldn't succeed at ending my life. As I looked out the window in the back seat, I hated everything around me. I wanted to die. I was sure that the last suicide attempt would have helped me accomplish that, but it didn't. Why was I still alive? I told myself that God was torturing me by keeping me alive and in my misery. In the back of my mind, I could hear my mom's voice. She was explaining how she had been at home and all of a sudden, she felt compelled to pray for me. She said that the more she prayed, the more of an urgency she felt. The urgency was so strong that she got to the point where she could no longer stay home. She felt compelled to come and check on me. She drove straight to my apartment. She said that she found me in my room, collapsed on the floor. She wasn't sure how long I had been there and she called 911. She insisted that God had once again spared my life because He had a greater and a better plan for my life. I didn't want to hear anything about God. I was so done with my life and living. I was definitely done with God and men too. I was tired of them letting me down and abusing me. I just wanted peace. I just wanted to go to sleep and never wake up again. When we pulled up to my apartment complex, I promised my parents that I wouldn't go anywhere and that I wouldn't drink. I told them I just wanted to be alone and needed my space.

That I night, I drank until I passed out again. I woke up about four in the morning with such an intense heaviness and deep sadness in me; it was worse than I had ever felt. I just lay in my bed and cried for a good hour until I was exhausted.

CHAPTER 13

A Moment of Clarity

This is where my story began. I was laying there in that bed, horrified and terrified of what was next in my life. As I lay there, all I could think was: *When will my suffering end?*

I reached for my bottle of vodka. As I unscrewed the top, I took a long hard drink and before it could even hit me, I hated myself all over again. I hated my failed life. As I lay in that bed, I tried to make sense of it all. I couldn't see any good left in my life. I looked over at the bed stand to see if I had any sleeping pills left, but I spotted a candle with the serenity prayer on it. A line on the candle leaped out at me. It read: "THE COURAGE TO CHANGE." That phrase hit me like a ton of bricks. *That's one thing that I lack*, I thought to myself. I definitely lacked courage. I was afraid of living and even attempting to get sober. I was afraid of the withdrawals from drugs and alcohol, but more importantly, I was afraid of how I was going to cope with the pain and hurt that was aching on the inside of me. Alcohol and drugs were the only things that gave me relief. They were my only means of escape. Without them to numb me, all the thoughts of my past would replay over and over in my mind. I didn't want to deal with the haunting memories and the feelings of anger, rejection and hurt. However, the very thing that was giving me temporary relief in one area of my life was killing me in every other area of my life. Thinking that it was just the liquor causing me to see the words the way I'd seen them, I tried to blink, hoping that the sobering thoughts would go away, but they remained. Something was going on; something was happening in that room. I could feel it. There was a change in the atmosphere and I could feel my mind getting clearer. I started reaching for the bottle of vodka again, but this time, I stopped. Immediately, my mind remembered what I was feeling; it was the presence of God. I sobered up almost immediately and spoke out loud, "God, is that you?" I felt a warmth come over my body and immediately, shame gripped me as I realized the presence of God had just entered the room and was surrounding me. I was hurt and broken, but most of all, I was very ashamed and dirty. I felt too sinful to be in His presence, but in that very same moment, there was a part of me that yearned for His love. That part of me cried out for it from the very core of my being. I was so dehydrated and dried up that as I much as I felt ashamed, the overwhelming desire to feel His love took precedence over my condemnation. Tears began to flow down my cheeks. "Oh God, I'm so sorry," I said. "Look at what a mess I have made of my life." I wept and cried. I knew that God was there and that I had two options: I could grab the life raft and jump on the boat with God or turn away and continue drowning in my misery. After being in His presence and remembering what His love felt like, the decision was an easy one, but I was still so afraid. Knowing my very thoughts, God spoke inside of me in a small, still voice. I'll never forget the words He uttered in my spirit. He said, "It's going to be one of the hardest things you'll ever do." I knew what He was referring to. He was dealing with my fear of getting sober and detoxing. Just the thought alone gripped me with fear. My drinking was beyond the point of me enjoying being drunk anymore. I was now drinking to numb the pain and the last thing I wanted to do was detox and go through that again. He went on saying, "But I promise, I will never leave you like every other man in your life has left you." Right then, something broke in me. I knew that what He was saying was the truth and the truth was literally setting me free in that very moment. Again, I told Him of my fears and He reassured me that He would be there through the entire process. I told Him that I was no good and I just didn't want to live anymore and He spoke so tenderly to me, "Cynthia, if you don't want to live anymore, that is fine. Don't live, but instead of taking your life, lay it down and give your life to me; die to yourself and live for me." I did not understand what that meant so I asked Him. I said, "God, what do you mean by dying to myself?" I don't know what that means. I didn't fully understand what it meant to die to myself, but in that moment, I did know that I was tired of living my life absent from God. Once I felt His presence again and experienced Him in an intimate way, my eyes were opened and immediately, everything in me was drawn to Him. In that moment, I decided that it didn't matter whether I understood what God was asking me to do; anything was better than the hell I had been living in. So right there in that room, I did something that I had never done in my life: I cried out wholeheartedly to God and I decided to surrender my will and my life back to Him. I told God to save me. I told Him that I received what He sent His Son to do for me on the cross and I expressed to Him that even though I didn't understand how He could make anything good out of my life, I no longer desired to live life without Him. Upon my decision to surrender my life, I saw a brightness fill my room. The closest way to accurately describe it is this way: it was as if prior to the presence of God entering that room, I was in the middle of a dark football field and upon the entrance of God's very presence, it was as if every light in the stadium had been simultaneously flipped on. The love that poured over me was overwhelming— to say the least. Knowing something had happened and knowing that this was the turning point for me (my moment of clarity), I immediately called my mom. I asked her to come get me. After work that day, she picked me up and took me to her home.

The Lord had spoken correctly; the next five days were dreadful and were worse than anything I could have imagined. My detox was horrific. I was hallucinating and saw things that terrified me: demons, snakes, and small creatures crawling along the walls. It felt as if there were bugs crawling all over my skin, but through it all, I felt safe and knew that my Abba Father was with me. He was not only with me, but proud of me. My parents were very supportive. They played Christian music in the room nonstop and prayed over me day and night, only leaving me when they had to go to work. My daughter was so happy that I was there and although she didn't completely understand what I was going through, she knew that something was different. I wasn't hiding from her and I wasn't drinking and that made her very happy.

CHAPTER 14

The Courage to Change

On the fifth day of my sobriety, my withdrawals subsided enough for me to get up without assistance and I was able to get cleaned up. When I had been in the women's recovery home right after the car accident, I remembered one of the women talking about a Christ-centered recovery program called "Celebrate Recovery." If there was one thing I knew, it was this: there was no way that I could ever remain sober without the Holy Spirit guiding me through the process. I looked up the address and opening hours of the closest Celebrate Recovery and within a couple of hours, I was walking into a meeting. I sat way in the back of the church building that the meeting was being held in. It was hard to sit still because I still had a bit of the shakes, plus, I was worried that someone would smell the alcohol that my body was still detoxing from through my

153

pores. For this reason, I sat far away from anyone. I searched for the woman I knew from the
recovery home. I spotted her towards the front of
the church, but I remained seated in the back.
That first meeting was one of the many that
would come in my future. This would become a
great place of healing for me. The women loved
on me and accepted me just as I was. I started attending another meeting on Sunday nights at The
Center Church, also known as Escondido Christian Center. I not only attended the Celebrate Recovery meetings there on Sunday night, but I also
went to their Wednesday night women's 12 step
group. It was a biblical study of the 12 steps of
Alcoholics Anonymous and Narcotics Anonymous. This is where I met my sponsor and dear
friend, Erika Caro. She and her husband, Alex, led
the Celebrate Recovery meeting. The first time I
encountered Erika, I didn't care for her too much
to be honest. I didn't like women at all. Due to my
deep insecurities, I perceived other women as a
threat to me, but her relentless love and the time
she spent pouring into me eventually broke
through the hard exterior shell that I had created
to protect myself from hurt. In our intimate

group, there were five women. By the leading of the Holy Spirit, Erika started helping me peel back the layers of my hurt and expose the root of why I was drinking, drugging and rebelling. I remember one particular breakthrough we had. She met with me away from the group at IHOP to work with me on one of my steps. It was there that I came to terms with the anger and resentment I was harboring towards myself and others.

Now, I would love to say that after my moment of clarity with the Lord that day in my bedroom, going to Celebrate Recovery and going through my twelve steps that I went on skipping through the tulips and lived happily ever after, but that is not my story. One thing that I have found in my journey is this: once I left that place, the altar was not my ending; it was my beginning. In my case, my altar was my bedroom because that's the place where I laid down my life, died to self, and gave myself entirely to the Lord. It's where my real fight began. I got free from a lot during my altar experience through receiving salvation, freedom from addiction, and an end to my rebellion. However, those things being removed in me exposed what was hiding beneath the hurt and addiction. God began to shed light on the many layers of hurt in me. Those tares that were deeply rooted in me that began when I was a little girl were now being exposed and I was staring at them face to face. God, being the loving God that He is, didn't want me to just find relief from my demons, He wanted to deliver me and set me free.

I found the next few months to be very difficult as I began to work through the layers ... I felt as if God was separating me from me and He was. He was exposing the old me and leading me into the new.

"For I am about to do something new. See, I have already begun! Do you not see it? I will make a pathway through the wilderness. I will create rivers in the dry wasteland."
Isaiah 43:19 (NLT)

I did see it, but the exposing of the old and the wasteland scared me. Even though I had much support from Erika and the other women in the group, I began to isolate myself, thinking that the mending of my past was too much for me to do. I didn't realize that God is the only one who can heal the brokenhearted, so I did what I always did when things got overwhelming to me: I ran. After I finished the 12 step group, I stopped attending Celebrate Recovery. I did this for a mixture of reasons. The first reason was fear. The next was an excuse. I have since found that these two jokers (fear and excuse) work hand in hand to keep us stuck at the threshold of our deliverance. (I hope you caught that!) My excuse was this: I had started taking a lot of classes at my local community college and told myself that I would not have time to serve at Celebrate Recovery and go to school full time. The very reason I had begun attending school was because I had tapped into an unknown gift in me to facilitate groups in Celebrate Recovery. This gave me the desire to go to college to get my degree and become a MFT (Marriage Family Therapist). The third reason was because of my own convictions regarding my lifestyle and behaviors outside of church and Celebrate Recovery. I felt like a hypocrite and here's why: I found myself leading two very different lives. I wasn't drinking, but I was what I call a "dry drunk." I hadn't relapsed, but I still had alcoholic behaviors. I would consistently go out every weekend to different nightclubs with my girlfriends. I felt lonely at home, so I would go out and dance, meet men, and more often than not, I would go home with one of the men I had just met. I had also joined a few online dating sites too. So if I wasn't at a nightclub, I was out on a date with a new guy. These two activities soon became my new addictions. The guilt of my behavior started consuming me to the point where I felt very ashamed. On Sundays, I was going to help lead a Celebrate Recovery group, talk about overcoming addictions and living a pure life by presenting your body to God as a living sacrifice, all the while, I was sleeping around and fornicating. I tried my best to justify it by saying that I was a grown woman with needs, but I knew deep down that my reasoning was not flying with God. There was also one single woman in the 12 step group who I had become very close to. Her name was Marlene and I desired to have the closeness that she had with the Lord. Her lifestyle convicted me so much. She would freely share with our group about her struggles in remaining pure and refraining from fornication, but her great desire to please God and her love for Him was what compelled her to continue in her walk of purity. The idea of purity, abstinence, and saving yourself for marriage was the craziest thought to me. It was hard enough for me to just refrain from having multiple partners in one weekend, so the thought of no sex at all was so unrealistic. The more conviction I felt, the further I withdrew myself from Celebrate Recovery, but not the Lord. I began to hate my behavior, but no matter how much I tried to stop, my need to be wanted, to feel attractive and to get attention from men (even the negative attention of a one night stand), overrode my disgust for my actions. Waking up next to a stranger while sober is a tough thing to do. That morning walk of shame into my home every weekend was sickening to me and I began to ask myself questions like: *Why do I do the very things that I hate and that makes me feel so much guilt?* Paul the apostle says in verse:

"I do not understand what I do. For what I want to do I do not do, but what I hate I do."

Romans 8:17 (NIV)

I would cry, pray and ask God questions like, "Why am I this way, Lord?" or "Why can't I stop seeking out men? Why do I need so much attention?"

"What a wretched man I am! Who will rescue me
from this body that is subject to death?"
Romans 7:24 (NIV)

Every time I met a nice guy who was genuinely interested in me, I wanted to be intimate with him immediately. After sex, he would lose respect for me for giving my body up so quickly and he'd dump me. This would break my heart and the spirit of rejection in me would get so stirred up that to prove to myself that I was beautiful and desirable, I would get dressed up, go out to a club and snag another man for the night to ease my pain. Unfortunately, this never eased the pain; it only made it worst. No one ever has a one night stand, wakes up the next morning in bed alone (after discovering that the gentleman has sneaked out of their bed and left) and says,

"Wow, that sure did make me feel loved and appreciated." It's quite the contrary. It made me feel even more empty, alone and filthy. What was even worse was on the seldom occasion that I tried not to be intimate with a man immediately upon meeting him, I would instead proceed to tie him down. I would try to get him to commit to a relationship with me when we had just started dating. This caused men to dump me or run for their dear lives because of their own fears of commitment and again, I would end up feeling rejected. So I was very needy, even though I covered it up pretty well. On the exterior, I appeared to be a tough, independent woman who had it all together, but that was just a facade to cover up the hurt, broken, and rejected little girl who was still living within me.

CHAPTER 15

Choose You This Day

In the midst of all this, I started dating a man (we will call him Luke). During a conversation, the subject of marriage came up. He told me that he desired to be married and that marriage was his overall goal in dating me. Instead of telling him that I was a basket case and in no way ready to get married, I pretended that I was everything he wanted in a wife. Instead of allowing God to continue working on me and allowing Him time and space to bring healing to me, I wanted a quick tangible fix. I wanted a man and I wanted to be married. I focused all my attention on my new relationship. I was so excited and truly thought that Luke would be the one I'd spend my life with (note: you can't love someone wholly from the place of your brokenness, unless that person is God). So what happened for me is this: I made Luke and our relationship my god. I put unrealistic expectations on him and it was very disappointing. I found it close to impossible to know how to function in a healthy relationship because I had never been in one. I was used to men being controlling and jealous. I was used to men being completely ridiculous in their attempts to demonstrate what they called love towards me. Luke wasn't clingy or needy and I took this as rejection. I would find myself completely overthinking even the vaguest harmless gesture from him and my life began to revolve around his next phone call, text or the next time I would see him. I would put on this façade that I didn't care one way or another if heard from him or not, but it was all an act. I tried my best not to be a stalker, but I would stalk him at any given chance. I would stalk his Facebook page, thinking that he had to be cheating on me. After that, I would think about what I was doing and feel like I was a crazy woman. Deep down in my heart, I feared that at any moment, he would find out that I wasn't good enough for him or worthy to be loved. And I worried that he would eventually find out I was a crazy, insecure stalker girlfriend and dump me like all the rest of the men in my life had, beginning with my father. This was full-fledged rejection and self-rejection in action. I didn't believe that Luke really cared about me and wanted me because I saw myself as undesirable and unworthy of real love. I hated feeling the way I did and acting out for no apparent reason, but even though I tried to stop, I could not.

One Halloween night, I was feeling lonely because I wasn't with Luke and one of my close friends (Monique) and I went out to the casino to a Halloween party. We'd met some really shady guys who'd tried to take advantage of us and after a few scary incidents with those guys, we managed to arrive home safely. I began thinking once again about the dangers of being out in some of the clubs and party scenes. Again, I began to question myself about why I felt compelled to be in those types of party scenes. Although, my partying lifestyle had subsided quite a bit since I started dating Luke, when I felt the slightest bit of loneliness, I was right back out there in the club. I was so sick of my behavior. That night, I had a dream that I was being chased by something or someone; I wasn't sure what or who, and in the chase, I got turned around and found myself lost. I found myself all alone in a wilderness. As I looked around in the wilderness for something that looked familiar, I came to a clearing in the brush and on the ground I saw a bottle of whiskey and a glass. I woke up knowing exactly what the dream meant. It had been almost four months since I'd attended Celebrate Recovery, had any contact with the women in my support circle or contacted my sponsor, Erika. She'd repeatedly reached out to me, but I was too ashamed of my actions to respond back to her. I knew that if I didn't get to a meeting immediately and reconnect with the people who loved and supported me, I was going to relapse and the fall would be a hard one. It would possibly be a fall that I would never recover from.

The next day was the Harvest festival at my mom's church. I volunteered to help out with the games and my friend, Monique, was there with her son. I told her that because of the events that transpired the previous night, along with the dream I had, I would no longer party or go out to any clubs. I also cut off all the men I was talking to on the dating sites. I decided that I would be monogamous and focus only on my relationship with Luke. The next day, I attended Celebrate Recovery and was welcomed with open arms. I knew that I should have never stopped attending. I also knew that if I was going to get strong spiritually, just attending the Celebrate Recovery meetings was not going to do it. I needed to start going to church faithfully and I needed to start putting God first in my life. This was very hard because of the prior "church hurt" I had experienced, but my desperation to get free, and not just sober, made me thirst for something more.

The following week, I attended my first Sunday morning service at The Center Church. I found a seat alone and proceeded to wait for the service to start. Everybody seemed to know each other and I knew no one. I was about to get up and walk out when I heard the Holy Spirit say, "Stay. Sit down. Be quiet and heal," and so I did. A visiting speaker from Nicaragua was ministering that day and his story touched my heart. He talked about his own story of rejection that came only seconds after he was born. His young mother, who was only age twelve years old at the time of his birth, was so scared that she threw him in an outhouse right after he was born. A young boy from the village, upon hearing his cries, fished him out of the fecal matter and saved his life. I was astonished at how he was able to overcome such rejection and that not only did he survive, but he was thriving in his life. He talked about how God called him back to that village and he was ministering to the people there. I wasn't sure what it was about him, but he seemed to have a freedom that I desired. I knew that I was saved and going to Heaven, but I wanted to be free while I was still alive. I knew that I wasn't free because I felt out of control in some areas in my life. My rejection had me bound to a lifestyle I despised and acting like a stalker in my relationship. Nevertheless, in this church service was a man who was rejected in every sense of the word and he was a living, breathing witness that not only could one get free from rejection but that God could use the very thing that caused the rejection to instill hope in others. In one portion of his message, he asked the congregation their thoughts on how he established his closeness with the Lord and how he came to realize the worth he had in Christ. He said that he prayed and asked God to remove anything and anybody from his life that stood between him and his relationship with God. He went on to say that when he did that, he was truly able to see who he was to God and he formed his identity out of that revelation and not what man thought of him. Oh, that sounded so good to me. So right there in that church service, I put my head down and prayed that exact prayer. Immediately upon saying that prayer, the Lord flashed a picture of Luke's face in my mind. "No, Lord!" I thought to myself. "Not him!" My thoughts raced as I realized that the Lord was showing me, in that very moment, what an idol I had made out of my relationship with Luke. He wanted me to end that relationship immediately because I had put Luke before Him. I walked out of the service knowing in my heart that I did not have the strength to do what God wanted me to do.

That evening, I prayed and asked the Lord why I had to break up with Luke. I shouted at the Lord that I had finally cut every other man out of my life from dating sites to Facebook. I had fully committed myself to this one relationship, only to have Him tell me to break it off. The Lord's response shook my very being. He answered me and said, "I told you to get off the dating sites and unfriend all of those men a long time ago, but you never did it for me. Cynthia, your desire to please Luke is greater than your desire to please me and I am a jealous God. I want all of your heart, so choose now: him or me." I wanted to choose God, but I was too scared to be alone. As I pondered what the Lord had just spoken to me, I came to the realization that since the age of thirteen years old, I had always had a boyfriend or several boyfriends. I didn't take any breaks between relationships or allow myself to have any time alone. This was since the age of thirteen; I always felt the need to have someone to feel loved and wanted. Even when I was married the first time, I didn't take a break between that marriage to heal. I immediately jumped into a second marriage while still enduring the process of divorce from the first. It was in that moment that I realized that my daddy issues had dictated almost every action and decision I made in my life and in relationships. When I realized this truth, I was not quite sure what to do, so I prayed this prayer. I said, "Lord, I want to be obedient, but I don't think I can do this on my own. I need your help." The following day, the relationship between Luke and I seemed to change from day to night. He stopped texting me and our nightly calls went unanswered by him. After three days of being ignored, I was distraught and I found myself crying on my bathroom floor, trying to figure out what was going on. At that moment, I wasn't sure what it was that I was most upset about: the fact that Luke was ignoring me or the way I was responding to him ignoring me. It was as if all my joy and all my happiness hinged on me getting Luke's attention and when he fell short, my peace, joy and happiness left. This brought the following scripture to mind:

"The thief comes only to steal and kill and destroy. I came that they may have life and have it abundantly."
John 10:10 (NIV)

I didn't feel like I had life more abundantly, yet the scripture clearly said that my Lord came

to give me life more abundantly. This means He
has given me freedom, but I wasn't feeling free
and I didn't look free. I looked bound. The enemy
had me in bondage and my fear was co-signing
with him. I was so afraid that Luke would leave
me just like my father had. I knew that if that
were to ever happen, it would hurt like hell. I was
so tired of experiencing hurt when all I wanted
was love. All the other men I had been in relationships with had ultimately ended up hurting
me. I was afraid that I was going to end up all
alone with no one to love me when I was old and
gray. Forgetting the prayer I had prayed just
three days earlier, I cried to God and asked Him
why this was happening. He responded with a
question. He asked, "I wonder if I asked you to
choose right now between him or me, who would
you choose?" It was at that moment that I realized the way Luke was treating me was a direct
manifestation of the prayer I prayed earlier that
week. I prayed and asked the Lord to help me to
disconnect from the relationship so that I could
be obedient to Him. Even though it was a tough
prayer to pray, I truly meant it. I sat on my bathroom floor in utter shock at the fact that the Lord

had answered this prayer. He changed Luke's heart to make the break up easier for me.

"Why God? Why do you want me to be all alone? Everyone else has a husband or a boyfriend in their life! Why can't I?" His response was the same as before. He repeated to me, "Who do you choose: me or this relationship?" My cries turned to frustration and after wrestling with the question for about five minutes, I shouted out, "FINE, LORD! I CHOOSE YOU! YOU HAPPY NOW? I WILL JUST LIVE MY LIFE ALL ALONE WITH NO ONE! I CHOOSE YOU! I LET GO OF THIS RELA-TIONSHIP AND I CHOOSE YOU!" I collapsed onto the floor like a runner does at the end of a race. I was exhausted and crawled to my bedroom and fell fast asleep.

The next morning, my daughter asked me if I was okay because she'd heard me crying and yelling the night before. I told her everything was fine. After I took her to school, I came back home and sat on my bed. I was heartbroken as I looked at my phone and saw no texts messages or calls from Luke. I looked up at the ceiling and before I could say a word to the Lord, I felt a wave of the most glorious feeling I had ever felt. Immediately, it took my mind back to that moment when God visited me in my bedroom; it was the same feeling. Pure love was enveloping me and it felt glorious, but I was somewhat confused as to why. The small still voice of the Lord began to speak to me. "My daughter, I'm so pleased with your obedience. You made a decision last night that you meant with all your heart and I'm so very pleased that you did." He then showed me a scene of an ocean. I was standing on the sand on the shore right where the tide would end. Then He said, "Never in your life have you ever crossed over this place with me. I would bring you to this place and ask you to step into the ocean with me , but every time I did, you would retreat in fear. Your fear of being alone and your fear that you might never receive the love you so needed and always wanted kept you returning to your vomit of toxic relationships and addictions. It kept you returning to the sins of your past and running into the arms of another man, but I am the Lord, your God, and I have the love you so desire and are in need of. Even if your father and every man in your life had loved you completely and fully, they still could never give you the love that you needed or desired because I created that need in you to only be filled by Me. Only I can fill it. I am a jealous God and I want all your heart, not some of your heart; I want ALL your heart. When I would reveal to you things that I wanted you to cut off or people you'd made idols of, you would always choose to please them over stepping into the ocean with me. But last night, you crossed over that place of fear and you have now stepped into a new place— a new territory with me and a new place in our relationship."

I realized that the love my Lord was speaking of and the love I was feeling at that very moment was the very love I had been seeking. He was telling me that not only had I found my true love, but that this love was readily available to me. From that moment on, my relationship with my Lord completely changed. A couple of days later, I finally had a conversation with Luke and he con-firmed what I already knew. He told me that ear-lier that week, he'd experienced a change of heart concerning us. He said he realized that even though things were going very well up until that point, that we were not a good match. The Lord had indeed changed the heart of that man. As I hung up the phone with Luke, I felt the tears well up in my eyes. The Lord spoke so clearly to me. He said, "Don't you cry or hold your head low for I have removed him from your life." So I obeyed and did just as the Lord had spoken.

CHAPTER 16

The Metamorphosis Begins

In the weeks that followed, I began the journey or process of my deliverance. I have since learned that deliverance is a process and even though some of us are at the very beginning of the process and some of us may be further along in the process, we are all being "processed" and "delivered" daily. Now, let me make this one thing clear: I had no idea in the beginning what deliverance was. I had never been to a deliverance conference, nor had I ever been taught about deliverance. My deliverance took place behind the closed doors of my bedroom, led by the Holy Spirit and it came about like this. First, the Lord asked me to do for Him what I had only done for men in the past. So, instead of getting up every morning, grabbing my phone and texting a man or making a phone call, I would come to the Lord in prayer and talk to Him. I would tell Him all the sweet things I had only said to men prior to my deliverance. You see, the way we behave and the habits we have weren't formed overnight, so when the Lord takes us through the process, it is not an overnight work. So, I would get alone with God and tell Him how awesome He was and how much I needed Him. I would tell Him that I was in love with Him and that I needed Him above anything a man could ever give me. In return, the Lord would meet me every morning and pour out His love for me. He would do this in such a tangible way that I became addicted to His love and our time together in prayer and worship. It was during these times of morning fellowship that I would hear Him speak things to me. When I would struggle with my feelings of loneliness and find myself falling into the same patterns or desiring to get into a relationship, I would stop and get alone with Him. When I wanted companionship, He would send someone to help me. He would bring godly women into my life; for example, Erika, my sponsor, was a great help to me. She was very encouraging in my walk and would speak life to me. Marlene was a great help as well. She would spend countless hours in prayer and teach me about living and walking in purity.

Another way God helped me in my process was by keeping me busy doing His work. I knew that I was not called to just sit, wait and hope for the day the Lord would say to me that I was now ready for marriage. I knew that some godly man would not just come galloping in on his horse and sweep me off my feet as we rode off into the sunset together. Those are just lies that Hollywood feeds us. So, I began to seek after what God wanted me to do with my life. What was it that I could do to serve Him? This came from a place of gratitude for all He had rescued me from. I was beginning to see the pieces of my shattered life coming together and they were forming the outline of a picture of His restoration. It was far from complete, but the mere picture stirred my gratefulness for the awesome God that I served. It also provoked my desire to serve Him and to give back to others. In my search to find what I was called to do, I realized the Lord had placed a compassion in for me for the people on the streets. I have a heart for the homeless and the broken. They were the ones who people didn't want to touch, let alone love on, nevertheless, God gave me such a compassion for them.

One day, while scrolling on Facebook, I saw a group of people who were doing what they called "Bags of Love" for the upcoming holidays. They were asking for volunteers to make gently used handbags filled with toiletries which could be given out to homeless women living on the streets. I immediately contacted the director and asked how I could get involved. He told me that each person was in charge of picking a team name and the area they wanted to give their bags out in. I was somewhat discouraged because I had no team. I was hoping to just help out on one of the existing teams, not create my own. So I prayed about the opportunity over the next few days and one night, I was leaving the grocery store with my daughter and there was an elderly woman huddled up in a corner, trying to get warm. Immediately, I could feel the compassion rise up in me. My daughter and I went right back into the store and bought the woman some hot tea, muffins, and a cup of noodles. I gave the items to her and she thanked me. I was feeling like I had done something great until I heard the Lord say, "She will eat up the tea, the muffins and the soup you gave her and will hunger again in a few hours. You have something that will sustain her and that is Me. I am the Bread of Life and the river that will never run dry. Tell her about me. Tell her that if she drinks of this well, she will never hunger or thirst again." I sat in my car crying at these words from the Lord. I had never ministered to anyone on the street before. I had a mental picture of me getting out of the car to minister to her and her throwing that hot tea at me. My daughter's voice interrupted my thoughts; she asked me why I was crying and if I was okay. "I'm fine, baby." I answered her. "Well mommy, are we going to go home?" she asked. I hesitated and then told her to wait there in the car and I would be right back. I went back over to the woman, ministered to her for about five minutes and told her what God had done in my life. I invited her to our church, prayed with her and hugged her. After that, I returned to my car. During the entire ten minute drive home, I was weeping so uncontrollably that I could barely see. My daughter kept staring at me. She was just as confused as I was about what was going on. When we finally parked the car in front of the house, I turned to look her in her eyes and I spoke these words to her. I said, "Lizzy, you know how broken mommy used to be, right?" She nodded her head in affirmation. "Well, God is calling me to go into the streets and help the people who are homeless, lost, and broken like mommy used to be. He wants me to help them, give them hope, and tell them about Him. He also wants us to give them something for Christmas. So this year, we aren't going to buy Christmas presents for each other. Instead, we are going to form a team of people to go and bless people out on the streets with some of the things they need and then tell them about Jesus." She just stared at me with her wide eyes. I proceeded to ask her, "So, are you in?" She looked a bit shocked, but then nodded her head in affirmation. Right there in the car, we made a "pinky promise" and a declaration to the Lord. We both said that we would be radically obedient to whatever God asked us to do.

The next day, I told my mom about the vision God showed me and she thought it was a wonderful idea. She said she wanted to join our team and our team grew from two people to three. The Lord gave me the name of our team: "His Love in Action." In the upcoming weeks, God's provision was overwhelming. People came from every direction to bring donations upon donations for the outreach. I still hadn't decided exactly where we would give out the bags of love or what shelter we should contact. A guy that I'd once briefly dated (we will call him Arthur) contacted me. He'd seen my posts on Facebook about needing volunteers and donations for the outreach. He used to live in downtown San Diego, but was currently living in Connecticut. He told me that there was a great need near where he used to live. He gave me some information and we began working together to figure out which shelter and area I should do the outreach. Our interest in each other was rekindled and because he was a Christian who loved the Lord with all his heart, I just knew that our relationship was put together by God and that he was "the one." For this reason, I dove right into another relationship without asking God for His opinion. We began working and praying together for the outreach, but we also spoke of future plans together. He was no longer living in San Diego; he had moved to Connecticut for work-related reasons, but that suited me just fine. I was busy working on the outreach and busy with holiday stuff so our rekindled relationship was put on the back burner. Howbeit, we continued to talk every day. When the date came around for our Bags of Love charitable event, we had over 15 volunteers and had collected about 150 Bags of Love, each stuffed with toiletries, snacks and a Bible in each purse. The distribution was one of the most awesome experiences I had ever experienced. I immediately knew that this was something that the Lord wanted me to do on a monthly basis. After the distribution, we gathered up the volunteers and they all agreed to help us in the upcoming year to keep the outreach going. I knew that I had found my niche and I was running with it.

The Sunday right before the following Christmas, our choir got up to sing and a woman sang the solo part. I didn't know her, but she had such a beautiful voice. As she sang, the Lord spoke to me. He told me that I was to get with that woman and allow her to disciple me. I didn't even know her name, but after the service, I found her and introduced myself. Her name was Natty. We took a picture together and I told her that I wanted to get with her and pray together at the start of the New Year.

In the days to come, I found myself battling in my relationship with Arthur. Looking back, I realize that there were a couple of reasons that we struggled. The first and main reason was that I wasn't ready to be in a relationship. I was still being processed. I was still learning how to stand on my own two wobbly legs and take baby steps in my walk with God. It was premature, but because he was a "good Christian man," I thought our relationship had to be arranged by God. Trying to balance my time with the Lord and give Arthur the time he desired was tough. Since we were long distance, our only means of communication were phone calls and text messages. I was extremely busy and still learning to spend time with the Lord consistently, so my communication with Arthur would often be the thing I neglected. He felt neglected and didn't seem to understand the relationship that I had with the Lord. Most of the time, I felt like I had to explain or defend why I did certain things in my relationship with the Lord and this put me on the defense. We were not on the same page spiritually and this caused a rift in our relationship. In the Celebrate Recovery groups that I lead, I often say that every person's relationship with the Lord is exclusive and unique like a fingerprint. No two people have identical fingerprints and no two relationships with the Lord are identical. A relationship is formed during intimate time with the Lord and through experience. Such was the case with Arthur and me; we were very different and when he tried to change or question my relationship with the Lord, I refused to conform or change to suit him. After all, I'd spent my entire life trying to please people and I was determined to not return to that vomit. This caused strife between us. The Lord's timing is very important. If I had waited, things wouldn't have went the way they did. If I had even asked the Lord and not assumed I was ready, I would not have found myself in a relationship that I was not yet ready for.

After a while, I started getting more resentful towards Arthur and he became frustrated with me. He started shutting me out. It was during these times that I started feeling lonely all over again. I started to question if our relationship was from God. The Word says in Luke 4:13 that the devil left until the next opportunity came. Seeing his opportune time, he came back and I started battling with the temptation to go out and hook up with any man just to rid myself of the loneliness that was haunting me. I wanted to go out to dinner with a man or even call a man and have a conversation so I could take my mind off the loneliness I was feeling. I had a deep desire to have a man to fill my time and reaffirm my worth. None of these things were necessarily wrong, but I was a person who used men as counterfeit gods. So, a part of my deliverance journey involved me learning to do what I should have been doing all along and that was to give God the place in my heart that I once gave to men. It wasn't easy. There would be some nights that temptation would come on so strong that I would be tempted to seek outside attention. Nevertheless, my loyalty to the Lord (not Arthur) stopped me from acting on those desires. So, instead of giving into the desires of my flesh, I would get alone in what I called my "homemade sanctuary" with The Lord. This consisted of lighting a bunch of candles and worshiping the Lord until the loneliness lifted. Because God is faithful, it lifted every time, but not without effort on my part. I would pour out my heart to God during these times. This is how I learned to deal with the turmoil I was feeling in the relationship. I didn't realize it then, but God was resetting my coping mechanism from man to Him. So the turmoil actually caused me to get closer to God. I began to use God like I once used drugs and alcohol to relieve my stress, feelings of worry, and deal with painful situations. He was always there and when He helped me through tough times, He added no sorrow with it.

A couple of days later, Arthur and I decided to arrange an in-person visit, hoping this would help out our relationship. We decided that I would fly out to visit him in Connecticut for my birthday in February. Our thoughts were that spending some time together in person would help ease some of the stress we both had been feeling in our relationship. I remember buying my plane ticket and purposely not asking God if I should go or not because I didn't want to hear the word "no." I just pretended everything was okay because he met the criteria; after all, he was Christian. He and I both had the same beliefs regarding premarital sex, so even though I was going to stay in his home, I would be staying in the extra bedroom. A couple of days after I purchased my ticket, I began having dreams about the visit. In those dreams, I would have an overwhelming sense that I had done something wrong and I felt so much shame and guilt. I would also have dreams that we were kissing and things got a bit out of control. I dismissed the dreams, but as the date of my departure to Connecticut approached, that unsettling feeling was so strong that I knew I couldn't fly out to see him. I remember breaking down, crying and asking the Lord to forgive me for not asking Him if I should go. The Lord put it on my heart to call him right then and tell him that I wasn't coming out for my birthday. Fear gripped me and I remember thinking that if I canceled, not only would I have a lonely birthday, but he would probably dump me for canceling on him. When I called Arthur to tell him that I wasn't going to come out, he was very upset. We both agreed that the relationship was over. We hung up the phone and I was devastated. I cried and asked God why it had to end this way. I really believed that he was the one for me. God proceeded to explain to me that even though Arthur was a Christian and did love Him, Arthur was my idea of who I thought God wanted for me. As I looked back over the past few months, I could clearly see what God meant, so I repented and asked the Lord to forgive me. I told Him that from that day forward, I wouldn't seek any other relationships besides my relationship with Him.

The following morning after breaking things off with Arthur, I went into my morning prayer. That's when I felt that same overwhelming sense of love and that feeling of God being pleased with my obedience to Him, just as I had when I broke off the previous relationship. I began to realize that with every big act of obedience or test I passed, my relationship with the Lord went to a new level. I decide that I would become so "about my Father's business" that when the time was right, the Lord would bring my husband into my life. However, I would stay out of it because my track record with men in the past was quite horrible.

CHAPTER 17

A Deeper Place

In the days to come, I experienced such a new level in my walk with the Lord; it was a deeper place.

Note: whenever there is a sacrifice of obedience made for the Lord, a breakthrough will follow. Anytime you die to self or place something that you cherish on the altar, in that place, you will see the Lord in a new way. This is demonstrated in Genesis 22, beginning in verse 1:

"After all this, God tested Abraham. God said, 'Abraham!' 'Yes?' answered Abraham. 'I'm listening.' He said, 'Take your dear son Isaac whom you love and go to the land of Moriah. Sacrifice him there as a burnt offering on one of the mountains that I'll point out to you.' Abraham got up early in the morning and saddled his donkey."
Genesis 22:1-3 (MSG)

Notice that the verse begins by saying that God was testing Abraham. God will test the intentions of our hearts, just like He had done to me with my past relationships. I had always failed the tests because I kept choosing to please men over God, but in this time of deliverance and processing, I was being retaught, retrained, and reset to choose God. This is similar to what Abraham went through. Notice in the third verse, it says that Abraham got up early in the morning to saddle his donkey. Where was he going so early? He was going to sacrifice his son. He didn't drag his feet or put off the trip for days, weeks, or months, all the while, asking God why He wanted him to kill Isaac. Instead, he was quick to obey God. This is because he trusted the Lord enough to obey His Word.

"Abraham took the wood for the burnt offering and gave it to Isaac his son to carry. He carried the flint and the knife. The two of them went off together. Isaac said to Abraham his father, 'Father?' 'Yes, my son.' 'We have flint and wood, but where's the sheep for the burnt offering?' Abraham said, 'Son, God will see to it that there's a

*sheep for the burnt offering.' And they kept on
walking together."*
Genesis 22:6-8 the (MSG)

Verse eight shows Abraham's trust in the
Lord. "God will see to it that there's a sheep for
the burnt offering."

*"They arrived at the place to which God had di-
rected him. Abraham built an altar. He laid out the
wood. Then he tied up Isaac and laid him on the
wood. Abraham reached out and took the knife to
kill his son. Just then an angel of GOD called to him
out of Heaven, 'Abraham! Abraham!' 'Yes, I'm listening.' 'Don't lay a hand on that boy! Don't touch
him! Now I know how fearlessly you fear God; you
didn't hesitate to place your son, your dear son, on
the altar for me.'"*
Genesis 22:9-12 (MSG)

Abraham had proven his loyalty to the Lord
by not withholding his own son— a son that he
and Sarah had waited a long time to have. He did
not hesitate to offer his own flesh and blood for
the Lord. I was beginning to understand what the

Lord meant when He told me on the day I returned to Him that I would need to die to myself to live for Him. The Lord was asking me, in those times of testing, to sacrifice even my very own flesh. He wanted me to die to myself, forsake the desires of my flesh and choose to obey Him instead. The very reason He required this was to bring me into a closer relationship with Him. Many times, we want the fruit of a close relationship with the Lord without the sacrifice. We want Him to trust us with more, but how can He do that when we won't obey Him in what we presently have?

"Abraham looked up. He saw a ram caught by its horns in the thicket. Abraham took the ram and sacrificed it as a burnt offering instead of his son. Abraham named that place GOD-Yireh (GOD-Sees-to-It). That's where we get the saying, 'On the mountain of GOD, he sees to it.'"
Genesis 22:13-14 (MSG)

After Abraham passed the test, he named that place "GOD-Yireh (GOD-Sees-to-It)." He saw a new facet of the Lord—a new part of His character that prior to the test, he had never experienced. His relationship and trust grew to a deeper place with the Lord so much so that He called God by a new name and God honored his obedience. Like I said earlier, every act of obedience brings new breakthroughs and new blessings.

"The angel of GOD spoke from Heaven a second time to Abraham: 'I swear—GOD's sure word!—because you have gone through with this, and have not refused to give me your son, your dear, dear son, I'll bless you—oh, how I'll bless you! And I'll make sure that your children flourish—like stars in the sky! like sand on the beaches! And your descendants will defeat their enemies. All nations on Earth will find themselves blessed through your descendants because you obeyed me.'"
Genesis 22:15-18 (MSG)

God wants us to live a life of active obedience to Him so that He can show Himself strong in our lives. He also wants to trust us with more. Trust me when I say if you pray and ask God for more, it's going to take sacrifice and testing.

"Behold, to obey is better than sacrifice, and to hearken than the fat of rams."
Samuel 15:22 (KJV)

As I sought the Lord more, I was over-whelmed by our relationship. I asked the Lord why it couldn't have been this way when I was in the ministry the first time. If I had experienced Him the way I was experiencing Him at that moment in my life, I would have stayed in ministry and never rebelled. He reminded me that at that time, I had not allowed Him to have a place in my heart to manifest Himself to me at that capacity. My life was too crowded with things, hurts, and the people I put before Him and He was pushed out by all the counterfeits.

"The eyes of the Lord search the whole earth in or-der to strengthen those whose hearts are fully committed to him."
2 Chronicles 16:9 (NLT)

The Lord explained the verse to me this way. The reason He has to search the earth for people whose hearts are fully committed to Him is because the buildings (idols) and superficial things in people's hearts are so built up around them that there is no room for Him. He can't even get to the door and knock on it, let alone come in and sup with them (Revelation 3:20). But when He does see a heart that has made room for Him and is open to Him, it's like a beacon of light amongst all the other hearts and it grabs His attention. He can enter in and show Himself strong through that vessel. After the Lord showed me this revelation, I worshipped Him in a very different way. I began to pray that He would remove any idols that I created or any hindrances that obstructed Him from having complete access to my whole heart. I began studying Malachi 3:3 about the Lord being a refiner's fire. During these studies, the Spirit of God would be so tangible that I would weep and cry out for hours. I knew there was something going on inside me, but I wasn't sure what it was. I remember describing it in one of my journal entries. I wrote that I felt like God was separating me in two. There was a ripping apart, almost like when you skin an animal— a separating of the very depth or center of who I was (character, mindsets, personality) from what

God was molding me into on the potter's wheel. I had never experienced this before, but it was extremely tough. I began to wonder if it was normal for me to feel this way. I prayed and asked the Lord to help me understand. Shortly after that prayer, I began to meet weekly with Natty— the sister from the choir. We began meeting together every week at a local coffee shop to pray. It was during those prayer times that I shared with her what I was experiencing in my time with the Lord. My sister, Natty, is such a seasoned woman of God and very knowledgeable in the Word. She gave me some very valuable information that helped me out a lot. I told her that during one of the times I was in prayer, I heard the word "soul ties," but I had no clue what they were. She gave me some YouTube links about the subject and explained to me how to do what the narrators on the videos said to. I followed through and prayed the prayers in my next prayer time and again, I would feel overwhelmed. I would start crying, sobbing and coughing. Additionally, I would feel as if something was shifting and moving inside my body. When I shared this with Natty, she gave me one of Apostle John Eckhardt's links on

YouTube entitled, "Mass Deliverance." A couple of days later, I had about ten minutes before my daughter was to be dismissed from school, so while I was in the car, I decided to play the link and see what it was about. Two minutes into it, I was crying uncontrollably and had to turn it off. I didn't understand why the things he was saying had moved me so much. I decided that I wasn't ready for that just yet. If I did listen to it in its entirety, it would be better for me to do in privacy and during a time alone with the Lord.

CHAPTER 18

Deliverance is My Portion

During my next prayer meeting at the coffee shop with Miss Natty, she extended an invitation for me to go with her to a three-day *Nurturing Your Purpose* conference in Whittier, California. That was to about three hours from where I lived. She told me that Apostle John Eckhardt (the gentlemen from the YouTube link she'd shared with me), was going to be the speaker. I still had not finished listening to the link, but everything in me told me to go to that conference. I hesitated at first to go. I wasn't sure how much it would cost and I didn't have any money. To my surprise, Natty said that she would cover the costs and even drive us up there. I gratefully accepted her invitation, in awe that this woman of God who I had only known a few weeks would sow into my life by paying my way. I was so excited to be going.

The night before the conference, I went into my "homemade sanctuary" and decided that I was going to play the mass deliverance link by Apostle Eckhardt. As it began to play, I almost immediately began crying, sobbing, coughing, and moaning. The moaning was like nothing I had ever experienced. It came from deep within me and as Apostle Eckhardt called out the different traumas, beginning with women who had been raped, rejection from the father, hurt, deep hurt, bitterness, anger, murder, wrath, unclean spirits and others, I literally felt as if I was being ripped in two. I remembered I had felt that same feeling once before during the prayer I prayed for breaking soul ties. The only way I can describe the feelings I experienced is —I felt like I was being separated or purged. I would later realize that this was true in the literal sense. I was being cleansed by the Lord's consuming fire. The Refiner's fire was burning out everything that was not from Him. I knew that God was delivering me at that moment. I knew that He was setting me free from everything that had kept me bound for most of my life. Deliverance was my portion and I ate freely of the children's bread.

I woke up the next morning feeling light and free. I couldn't wait to go to the conference and get more teaching, word, and time with the Lord. Nothing could have prepared me for what I was about to experience. From the moment we walked into the conference, I felt the Holy Spirit like never before. I had never experienced being in that type of atmosphere where the apostolic anointing was present. What is the apostolic? Apostle means "sent one." The Holy Spirit is an apostolic spirit. The Spirit of God has been sent to us (Galatians 4:6). Jesus Christ was sent by the Father. Jesus turned His disciples into apostles when He said, "As the Father has sent Me, so send I you" (John 20:21). Apostolic people are sent into an area to war against demons, to deliver people from bondage, and to serve God. Apostolic people focus on the Kingdom of God with singleness of vision (1 Corinthians 15:58). They submit to the Word for their desire is holiness and for the sound doctrine of the the true gospel to be spread. They submit to the fire of God for cleansing, purging, deliverance from evil (2000 Mary Craig Ministries, Inc.).

The next three days of worship, teaching, impartations and prophetic words changed me in such a mighty way. John Eckhardt, operating in the office of an Apostle, carried that anointing on his life and I received it on my life by impartation that weekend. I came home so encouraged and excited for my future. My vision was so clear about what God wanted me to do and I wasn't afraid to walk into it. I was free and I wanted to get everyone else free! That's another attribute of the apostolic anointing; it is an anointing that builds and plants.

I felt that while I was there, I had been set on the right path. My feet literally felt planted and a new boldness had risen up in me. That anointing had broken the power of hindering spirits and confusion, and it set my destiny in motion. My life was completely changed.

In the months to come, I would see the favor of this apostolic anointing in action in my life. Doors began to fly open for me. I stayed in the Word and began reading good deliverance books. I also read books on the prophetic. I listened to teachings via YouTube and Periscope and gleaned all I could on these topics. I learned about living a life of deliverance and how to do spiritual warfare on behalf of my family and myself. I learned how to walk in my God-given power and authority. I became aggressive in the way I prayed. I was done being passive with the devil. I learned to stand against the enemy when I was tempted to partake in old behaviors. I learned how to resist when my flesh wanted to re-open doors that once allowed entrance to demonic spirits. I learned that deliverance is not a one-time event; it must become a lifestyle in the life of a believer. After the altar or post-deliverance is where the real work begins. One has to maintain their freedom from demonic spirits. In place of where demonic spirits once dwelt, I was now filled with the Holy Spirit and to stay filled, I would need to submit myself to the Word of God and apply it to my life daily. I had to learn to live a life of purity and holiness; I had to crucify my flesh and walk after the Spirit. To return to my old behaviors and wrong actions would make deliverance of null effect in my life and bring a worse state on myself than before.

"When an impure spirit comes out of a person, it goes through arid places seeking rest and does not find it.
Then it says, 'I will return to the house I left.' When it arrives, it finds the house unoccupied, swept clean and put in order.
Then it goes and takes with it seven other spirits more wicked than itself, and they go in and live there. And the final condition of that person is worse than the first."
Matthew 12:43-45 (NIV)

I knew that staying and cultivating one's relationship with the Holy Spirit is detrimental for living a life that's free indeed—just as salvation must be a lifestyle as well. It may initially take one act to come to the altar to be saved, but when we sin after our altar experience, we must come to God and repent. We must ask Him for forgiveness of sins committed again, and again and again— not just the one initial time.

The Lord told me to attend a few conferences that were coming up. I had a burning desire in me to do the ministry of deliverance on anyone who desired to be free; I wanted to get hands-on training. At these conferences, I was activated prophetically and in deliverance. I began doing deliverance with my family members. I started telling Erika, Marlene and other ladies about deliverance and how it had changed my life. Before long, everyone was getting free and everyone was prophesying. I was watching the Lord completely change, not only my life, but the lives of my friends and family members. It was such a beautiful work of the Lord. There was such a new boldness in me. I had never felt that type of boldness before, but the spirits of timidity and shame had been completely broken off my life. I was no longer apprehensive to speak or ashamed of the gospel.

Every last Saturday of the month, our homeless outreach program (His Love in Action) was in full swing. God's hands were upon it and people would just volunteer freely and donate generously to it. They would give of their time and give financially. I was going boldly into the streets of downtown San Diego, along with my volunteers, ministering to those bound in addiction, prosti-

tution, and poverty. I was laying hands, prophesying, and preaching to them. I know that this is
what God has called me to do.

My Aunt Norma, who now pastors a church in
the city I lived in, invited me to come speak at her
Women's Valentine Tea. Other than to the groups
in Celebrate Recovery, I had not spoken publicly
since I was in the ministry some ten years prior. I
was a little nervous, but I knew the Lord had a
Word in me that He wanted me to release to the
women. My pastor's wife was at the tea that day.
After the tea was over, she left me a message asking if we could meet for a brief meeting in the
next day or two. I agreed, but was not sure what
the meeting could possibly be about. The next
Sunday, right before the service was about to
start, my Pastor pulled me aside after prayer. He
told me that his wife enjoyed the message I
preached at the tea and he asked me if I would
pray about ministering to the congregation on
Mother's Day during the Sunday morning service. I was both shocked and honored. I told him
that I would pray about it and let him know. A
few days later, I met with my Pastor's wife. I was

expecting to go over the details of the upcoming Mother's Day service, but to my surprise, she only briefly mentioned Mother's Day. She disclosed to me the reason for our meeting was that she had been praying about who they should allow to lead the women's ministry at the church. The current leader was stepping down and she told me that after hearing me minister at the tea, God placed it on her heart to offer the position to me. After praying about ministering on Mother's Day and taking on leading the women's ministry at our church, I happily accepted both. I was taken aback at how quickly God was moving in my life but, at the same time, I had such a peace about what the future held.

CHAPTER 19

Prodigal Daughter Returns

Mother's Day morning was such an awesome demonstration to me of God's goodness. I had a special word for the mothers and all who were present and willing to receive that day. I spoke openly and transparently about my life's journey, along with all the mistakes I made along the way. I gave glory to my Savior for healing my broken heart and setting me free. I spoke of how He wanted to do the same for all who were present in that service. God moved in a mighty way in that place and many were set free. That morning was a perfect picture of God's restoration in my life. As I looked out into the congregation while I was ministering, I saw my mother and stepdad on the front row, weeping tears of joy as I told my story. As I looked on, I saw my sons and daughter looking at me with such honor in their eyes at the woman God had transformed their mother into. I saw my Uncle Daniel and Aunt Norma (the pastors who'd stood up and spoke in court to the judge on my behalf when I faced prison time). They once pleaded my case before for the judge and pleaded to God to have mercy on me. I saw my best friend, Monique, who'd cared for me many nights when I was sloppy drunk and no one else wanted to be bothered with me. These people had all loved me when I was unlovable. Now, they were all present in that church, watching the fruits of their labor in full bloom. Erika was there cheering me on, along with the ladies who were in my twelve step class. They'd watched me transform from the broken woman with five days into sobriety into one who had been set free. I was now free indeed. My pastor was there. He'd preached the Word without compromise, taught me the true love of a shepherd, and loved me back into the family of God. My pastor's wife was there. She'd seen God's potential in me and she'd stepped out on faith by giving me the opportunity to lead the women's ministry. They were all in that room and once again, I was so unspeakably grateful to God for what He had done in my life.

When I surrendered to God the day that He visited me in my bedroom, I thought that the miracle would be that I would somehow remain sober. I thought He was saving me from drinking myself to death and giving me the opportunity to live a decent life, nevertheless, His plan was and is so much greater!

So, I say to you— the one who is reading this book right now: you are not reading this by coincidence. I want you to know that there is never anyone who is a lost cause with God. Don't you ever believe the lies of the enemy when he tells you that it's too late for anything good to come from your life or that you have made too many mistakes in your past to be used by God. I am living proof that God is in love with those who are messy, broken, addicted, unfaithful, and rebellious. His love for us is relentless and like a lovesick partner, He chases us down and pours out His love on us. He makes it completely impossible to not to fall in love with Him, and all He wants in return is our hearts. What He did for me, He can and will do for you if you let Him. All He needs you to do is come to the altar (a homemade altar works just fine), surrender your life to Him, die to yourself, and live for Him. If you do that, I can guarantee you that He will do a miracle with the broken pieces of your life. Do you know how I know this? Because He used this girl that was once:

- abandoned
- raped
- abused and beaten
- was a baby having babies
- served in the ministry and then turned her back on the call and her Lord
- lived eight years of a life riddled with addiction and full of rebellion.

That woman came to herself while in her pit and returned to her Father as the Prodigal Daughter. Even though she was willing to merely be a hired servant or slave in Her Father's house, His plans for her were far more. Oh yes, He greeted her with open arms and received her—He never rejected her. He cleaned her up and covered her with His presence like jewels adorning the finest robe. He blessed her and put a ring for her finger, declaring His covenant with her. He put sandals on her feet, which meant that she would no longer wander. From that point on, her every step would be ordered by Him. He celebrated her with a feast and claimed her as His daughter, declaring that she was indeed once dead in her sins, but now, has returned to life in Him. She was once lost but now, she is found. So the party has begun and to this day, that girl continues to be used for her Father's glory. She is His "sent one," designed to bring the message that Jesus preached in Luke 4:18-19:

"The Spirit of the Lord is upon me, because he hath anointed me to preach the gospel to the poor; he hath sent me to heal the brokenhearted, to preach deliverance to the captives, and recovering of sight to the blind, to set at liberty them that are bruised."

....and that girl is me.

CPSIA information can be obtained
at www.ICGtesting.com
Printed in the USA
FSOW03n2135060217
30504FS

9 780998 250762